TRADING
OPTIONS
AT
EXPIRATION

TRADING OPTIONS

AT

EXPIRATION

STRATEGIES AND MODELS FOR WINNING THE ENDGAME

JEFF AUGEN

Vice President, Publisher: Tim Moore
Associate Publisher and Director of Marketing: Amy Neidlinger
Executive Editor: Jim Boyd
Editorial Assistants: Myesha Graham, Pamela Boland
Operations Manager: Gina Kanouse
Digital Marketing Manager: Julie Phifer
Publicity Manager: Laura Czaja
Assistant Marketing Manager: Megan Colvin
Cover Designer: Chuti Prasertsith
Managing Editor: Kristy Hart
Project Editor: Betsy Harris
Copy Editor: Keith Cline
Proofreader: Kathy Ruiz
Indexer: Erika Millen
Compositor: TnT Design
Manufacturing Buyer: Dan Uhrig

© 2009 by Pearson Education, Inc.

Publishing as FT Press

Upper Saddle River, New Jersey 07458

This book is sold with the understanding that neither the author nor the publisher is engaged in rendering legal, accounting or other professional services or advice by publishing this book. Each individual situation is unique. Thus, if legal or financial advice or other expert assistance is required in a specific situation, the services of a competent professional should be sought to ensure that the situation has been evaluated carefully and appropriately. The author and the publisher disclaim any liability, loss, or risk resulting directly or indirectly, from the use or application of any of the contents of this book.

FT Press offers excellent discounts on this book when ordered in quantity for bulk purchases or special sales. For more information, please contact U.S. Corporate and Government Sales, 1-800-382-3419, corpsales@pearsontechgroup.com. For sales outside the U.S., please contact International Sales at international@pearson.com.

Company and product names mentioned herein are the trademarks or registered trademarks of their respective owners.

Printed in the United States of America

Second Printing May 2009

ISBN-10: 0-13-505872-4
ISBN-13: 978-0-13-505872-5

Pearson Education LTD.
Pearson Education Australia PTY, Limited.
Pearson Education Singapore, Pte. Ltd.
Pearson Education North Asia, Ltd.
Pearson Education Canada, Ltd.
Pearson Educación de Mexico, S.A. de C.V.
Pearson Education—Japan
Pearson Education Malaysia, Pte. Ltd.

Library of Congress Cataloging-in-Publication Data

Augen, Jeffrey.

  Trading options at expiration : strategies and models for winning the endgame / Jeff Augen.

    p. cm.

  ISBN 0-13-505872-4 (hardback : alk. paper) 1. Options (Finance) 2. Investment analysis. 3. Securities—Prices. 4. Stock price forecasting. I. Title.

  HG6024.A3A9226 2009

  332.63'2283—dc22

                                           2008051445

*To Lisa—the most independent person I know—
who taught me never to rely on anyone for
anything. I only made it this far because of you.*

Contents

Acknowledgments

I'd like to thank everyone who helped turn some good ideas and a few words on paper into a complete book. Foremost is Jim Boyd who first had the idea of a single-topic options trading book. The work would never have taken form without Jim's input.

Authors write words and make charts, but finished books are created by project editors. Once again it has been my pleasure to work with Betsy Harris who created a publication-quality document from a rough draft. In that regard I would also like to thank Keith Cline who patiently edited the original text.

Authors rarely step back and take an objective look at their own work. That task fell to Robert Balon and Michael Thomsett, who read every word and contributed valuable ideas. Their comments and enthusiasm for the material gave me confidence that helped shape the presentation.

Finally, I would like to acknowledge the excellent work of the Pearson marketing team and especially Julie Phifer, who always seems willing to put real thought behind new book concepts.

Writing this book and working with a team of focused professionals has been a real privilege. Our goal has been to produce a true source of value creation for the investment community in these turbulent times.

About the Author

Jeff **Augen**, currently a private investor and writer, has spent over a decade building a unique intellectual property portfolio of databases, algorithms, and associated software for technical analysis of derivatives prices. His work, which includes more than a million lines of computer code, is particularly focused on the identification of subtle anomalies and price distortions.

Augen has a 25-year history in information technology. As a cofounding executive of IBM's Life Sciences Computing business, he defined a growth strategy that resulted in $1.2 billion of new revenue and managed a large portfolio of venture capital investments. From 2002 to 2005, Augen was President and CEO of TurboWorx Inc., a technical computing software company founded by the chairman of the Department of Computer Science at Yale University. He is the author of three previous books: *The Option Trader's Workbook* (FT Press 2008), *The Volatility Edge in Options Trading* (FT Press 2008) and *Bioinformatics in the Post-Genomic Era* (Addison-Wesley 2005).

Much of his current work on option pricing is built around algorithms for predicting molecular structures that he developed many years ago as a graduate student in biochemistry.

Introduction and Explanatory Notes

Timing

This book was written during one of the most turbulent times in stock market history—the second half of 2008. During this time frame, trillions of dollars were lost by both bulls and bears as the world's financial markets "melted down." Investors who have never experienced a crashing market often believe that it is easy to generate profits in this environment with short positions. Unfortunately, nothing is ever that simple. The 2008 collapse included single-day bear market rallies as large as 11%—large enough to destroy nearly any short position. The answer lies in reducing market exposure and trading only when it makes sense.

Far too many investors have taken the opposite approach by remaining in the market with a portfolio of investments whether they were winning or losing. This approach has its own familiar vocabulary built around terms such as *value investing* and *diversification*. It hasn't worked well for most investors. At the time of this writing, U.S. equity markets had just plunged to their 1997 levels, erasing 11 years of gains. Subtracting an additional 30% for inflation and dollar devaluation paints an even darker, but more realistic picture. As a group, long-term stock investors collectively lost an enormous amount of money—trillions of dollars.

Commodity traders faced similar problems. Oil prices climbed steeply from $27 in January 2004 to $134 in July 2008 before falling back to $50 in November. Long-term bulls actually suffered two significant setbacks during this time frame because the price fluctuated from an interim high of $70 in August 2006 to a low of $45 just five months later. Figure I.1 traces the price from January 2004 through the November 2008 decline.

As always, timing is everything. But the more important lesson is that blindly hanging on with a bullish or bearish view is a flawed strategy. Every investment has a window of opportunity; unless that window can be identified, leaving the money invested is somewhat like gambling. That said, the window can be relatively long—sometimes spanning months or years.

Option trading in turbulent times can also be difficult. Implied volatilities rise sharply, making simple long put or call positions unreasonably expensive, and the risks associated with naked short positions is simply too large for any conservative investor. Structured positions such as calendar spreads, ratios, vertical spreads, and the like, are difficult to trade because stocks frequently cross several strike prices in a single month—sometimes in both directions.

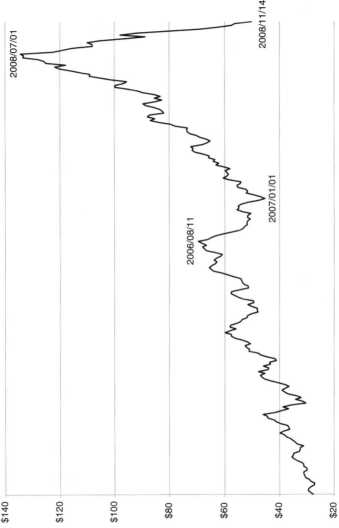

FIGURE I.1 *Weekly U.S. spot price for crude oil 2004/01/02 to 2008/11/14. Price is displayed on the y-axis, key dates are noted on the chart. Source: U.S. Department of Energy, Energy Information Agency, www.eia.doe.gov.*

These pitfalls can all be avoided by entering the market at very specific times and structuring trades that capitalize on well-characterized pricing anomalies. For option traders, the days preceding expiration represent the very best opportunity. During this time frame, traditional approaches to calculating the value of an option contract fail, and prices become distorted. One of the most significant forces, implied volatility collapse, can generate price distortions as large as 30% on expiration Thursday and 100% on Friday for at-the-money options. At the same time, strike price effects resemble the gravitational pull of planets, with stocks as their satellites. Heavily traded optionable stocks tend to hover around strike prices as large institutional investors unwind complex positions ahead of expiration. Option traders who structure day trades that take advantage of these forces can generate more profit in one day than most experienced investors realize in an entire month—sometimes an entire year.

Unlike other trading strategies that are linked—sometimes in subtle ways—to a specific set of market conditions, expiration trading focuses only on the underlying mathematics. It does not rely on any financial predictions, company results, or market direction. In this context, an expiration trader manages ticker symbols and strike prices because the name or business of the underlying stock is irrelevant. But nothing worth doing is ever easy. Trading subtle price distortions in the options market is a complex affair that requires an unusual blend of pricing knowledge and day trading skill. Expiration trading is a mathematical game distinctly different from stock picking. It will most likely appeal to day traders and other investors seeking to moderate risk by reducing market exposure. That said, this book should never be placed in the "get rich quick" section of the bookstore because success requires hard work, focused attention, and practice.

Some Notes About the Data

A relatively large amount of minute-by-minute stock and option data was used in the preparation of this book. This information, in its unprocessed form, was purchased from Tick Data of Great Falls, Virginia. Many specific criteria went into the decision to choose this particular data source.

First, and most significant, was accuracy. Because slight discrepancies can cause significant errors in implied volatility calculations, it is important that the data be both accurate and complete. Assembling complete and accurate datasets is not a trivial exercise, as options trade on several different exchanges, often at low liquidity levels. It is, therefore, necessary that the data vendor precisely align timestamps for the individual trades before creating a single sequence or time series. In addition, the large number of strike price and expiration date combinations adds a level of complexity that becomes apparent when a new series is introduced or a stock splits. This situation is further complicated by the enormous number of symbols used and reused by the options market. When creating data files of option prices, it is, therefore, crucial that old and new data or data from different equities not be mistakenly commingled despite the presence of overlapping symbols. In this regard, it is not unusual for a single stock in a given year to have more than 1,200 strike price/expiration date combinations. Multiplying by the number of stocks and years yields a very large number of permutations.

File format is another important criterion. Individual files should contain text delimited by commas, spaces, or some other readily identifiable marker so that the information can be imported into a database or spreadsheet. Filenames should follow a consistent set of conventions that make it simple to identify a particular series. For example, trade data for the Apple Computer $170 strike price call expiring on 2010/01/16 and having the symbol WAA_AN might be stored in a file designated WAA_C_20100116_170.00_AN. This file can easily be found using Excel's import feature by searching for the concatenated expiration strike (20100116_170). The search will yield just two files, one containing call data, and the other containing put data (the put file would be designated WAA_P_20100116_170.00_MN). In this way, simple file-retrieval functions found in Microsoft Office products can be used to retrieve an individual option series from tens of thousands, and the collection of files effectively becomes a database.

Tick Data files were named as described above, and the information was provided as simple comma-delimited text. The data was clean in the sense that series designations were consistent and anomalies that made no sense were removed. In this context, the term anomalies refers to trades that were made in error—an option purchased for $125 rather than $1.25. Furthermore, time series used in the book were spot checked by calculating implied volatilities across multiple strike prices contained in different files. No inconsistencies were found in any of the Tick Data information. Readers who decide to purchase their own data are encouraged to apply the same level of scrutiny before selecting a vendor.

Working with Minute-by-Minute Data

Expiration trading provides enormous opportunities that scale with the amount of time and effort an investor is willing to spend. It is certainly reasonable to study options expiration by observing the behavior of individual stocks, and to profitably trade the opportunity using principles outlined in these pages. That approach represents one end of the spectrum. The other end involves the development of custom databases and software. Although most investors are probably not inclined to build their own databases, many will discover that much of the statistical analysis mentioned in these pages can be compiled with little effort and no programming using the capabilities of Microsoft Excel. Following are a few simple examples.

The first, and probably most relevant for the present discussion, is the determination of the nearest strike for each closing price. This value can be determined for stocks having $5 spacing using Excel's rounding function, as follows:

```
Strike = (ROUND (Close /5)) *5
```

Assuming that each line of the spreadsheet contains data for a single minute, the formula can simply be pasted down a column of the sheet to create a running list of nearest strikes. Adding another column that calculates the difference between strike and closing prices takes just a few moments. The calculation would use the absolute value function:

```
Difference = ABS (Strike - Close)
```

Extending this operation with a simple conditional if/then statement enables us to determine the number of minutes where the closing price was more than $2 from the strike price. The following statement marks rows that exceed the $2 threshold with the number 1:

```
If (ABS (Strike - Close) > 2, 1,"")
```

As before, pasting the formula down the spreadsheet automatically marks all appropriate rows. Summing the results and dividing by the number of minutes (rows) gives the percentage chance of any minute closing more than $2 from a strike.

Finally, we can execute more powerful conditionals without adding much complexity using Excel's AND, OR, *and* NOT functions. Marking and counting the number of minutes containing a strike cross can be accomplished as follows:

```
If (AND (High>Strike, Low<Strike),1,"")
```

As before, summing the column yields the total number of minutes meeting the criterion—in this case, a strike price cross. The design assumes that only one strike price will be crossed in a single minute—an assumption that turns out to be true virtually 100% of the time. More complex logical structures can be designed for situations where a single record can contain multiple strike price crosses; the general case, designed for any length record, is best deployed as part of a program linked to a database. A fully functional example written in Excel VBA is listed in Appendix 1, "Excel VBA Program for Counting Strike Price Crosses."

These examples represent only a tiny fraction of the statistical queries that can be constructed in just a few minutes using minute-by-minute data imported into a spreadsheet. Surprisingly, this capability is relatively new; older versions of Excel (pre-2007) were limited to approximately 65,000 rows per worksheet—less than a single year of minute-by-minute data. Before the introduction of Office 2007, large amounts of information could be managed only by using a database and custom software. The combination of fast multiprocessing desktop computers and large-capacity spreadsheets now makes it reasonable for nearly anyone to purchase and analyze very large datasets. Current Excel worksheets can handle more than 1 million rows and 16,000 columns.

Ambitious investors with programming experience will want to take the next step by constructing databases and writing custom software. The information used throughout this book was stored in a database constructed with Microsoft SQL Server. The complete database contains millions of records along with custom programs and SQL queries. Despite its complexity, none of the work is beyond the capabilities of a determined investor with a desktop PC and Microsoft Office software. Furthermore, single-user versions of Oracle and IBM DB2 databases are also available for free download from company websites. These "developer" versions are very powerful and can be expanded to full corporate licenses with unlimited storage capacity and advanced security features.

Additional Notes Regarding Collateral Requirements and Pattern Day Trading Rules

Many of the trades described in these pages are structured as ratios where a certain number of options are purchased at one strike price and a larger number sold at a more distant strike. For example, a call ratio spread consisting of 10 long $95 calls and 20 short $100 calls would be referred to as a 1:2 call ratio. Many of our discussions use a larger ratio—most typically 1:3. Each of these trades has a naked short component because more options are sold than bought. The naked short component has a collateral requirement equal to 100% of the option proceeds plus 20% of the underlying security value minus the amount that the option is out-of-the-money. For $105 strike price calls costing $2.50 on a stock trading at $97, the calculation for a single contract would be as follows:

Option proceeds	100 × $2.50 =	$250
Underlying stock	20% × 100 × $97 =	1,940
Out-of-the-money adjustment	($105 – $97) × 100 =	(800)
Total		1,390

Because the adjustment for out-of-the-money options can be very large, a minimum of 100% of the option proceeds plus 10% of the underlying security value applies. Throughout the book when profits are mentioned, they are measured against the value of the original position, and collateral requirements are not included. For example, if a trade is long $5,000 of options and short $4,000, then the initial net cost of the trade is just $1,000. If the trade is ultimately closed for $1,500, the gain is considered to be $500 or 50%. Critics will rightfully point out that the return should be calculated using the collateral cost because this money must be present in the account while the trade is open. I have intentionally avoided this comparison because collateral requirements vary between brokers for different customer accounts.[1] In addition, for customers who are able to take advantage of portfolio margining, the requirement for a particular trade depends on other positions in the account. It is generally a good idea to understand the collateral requirements for your own account, and to keep these in mind when placing short trades.

One additional requirement to keep in mind is the SEC 2520 Pattern Day Trader rule, which requires day traders to maintain account balances of at least $25,000. In this regard, the term *pattern day trader* refers to an investor who executes four or more "round-trip" day trades within five business days. The strategies outlined in this book are, therefore, not appropriate for accounts smaller than $25,000 because they involve opening and closing the same position during a single trading session.

Endnotes

1. Recent changes allow customers whose accounts exceed certain minimum thresholds to take advantage of portfolio margining rules that more precisely align collateral requirements with overall portfolio risk. Readers wanting to further explore margin and collateral requirements are encouraged to visit the Chicago Board Options Exchange website and to contact their broker.

Chapter 1

Expiration Pricing Dynamics

E quity and index options expire on the third Friday of each month.[1] The final hours of each expiration cycle are characterized by unusual market forces and price distortions that, properly exploited, provide outstanding trading opportunities. These distortions are caused by the breakdown of traditional option pricing calculations that depend on volatility and time decay to fairly represent risk. As a result, options are unavoidably mispriced during the final few days.

End-of-cycle price distortions represent a market inefficiency that cannot easily be exploited by large institutions for reasons related to liquidity and execution efficiency. The trading strategies outlined in this book scale to hundreds, but not thousands, of contracts. Institutions normally trade thousands, tens of thousands, or even hundreds of thousands of contracts in structured positions that must be capitalized through a lengthy pricing process. These dynamics are best suited to private investors trading online with accounts that range from $50,000 to no more than $10 million—an order of magnitude smaller than most institutional accounts.

This approach to trading offers three compelling advantages: a reduced risk/return profile, limited market exposure, and extremely high returns on a percentage basis. In addition, the focus on price distortions and market anomalies makes for a direction-neutral strategy that doesn't rely on the investor's ability to "pick stocks." We explore a variety of trades that typically return anywhere from 40% at the conservative end to as much as 300% at the high end. In point of fact, just a few days before these words were written—at the April 2008 expiration—the exchange-traded fund OIH opened at $200 with the $200 straddle trading for approximately $2.50. By 12:00 the stock had climbed to $208, and the straddle was worth more than $8.00—a 220% profit. Stated differently, every $10,000 invested grew to $32,000. This sort of behavior is the norm on expiration day when stocks move from one strike to another and options are very inexpensive. More important, an investor who purchased this straddle risked only a modest amount of steady time decay. A typical expiration Friday presents several such opportunities.

In all cases, because we are actively trading these positions in real time with no intention of taking any options home after the close, there is little risk of losing money. Discipline is the key, and, as always, losing positions should be closed or adjusted.

Market Forces

End-of-cycle effects that are not comprehended by contemporary pricing models fall into three categories:

- Implied volatility collapse on the final trading day
- Strike price effects, including "pinning"
- Rapidly accelerating time decay

Implied Volatility Collapse

Collapsing volatility is a major driving force on expiration Friday. Early in the day, stocks still have 6.5 hours of normal trading time left and more than 38 hours before option contracts expire. Implied volatility is normally consistent with recent historical volatility. However, at the market close, more than one full day still remains before expiration. If implied volatility remained relatively high, out-of-the-money options would have unrealistic prices, and brokers would not purchase in-the-money options for Saturday exercise. For example, when priced with 42% implied volatility, at-the-money options on a $100 stock would still be worth more than $1.00 at the close. This price would be unrealistic for options that can no longer be traded by public customers. A trader, institutional or public, who purchased these options for Saturday exercise would be gambling that the stock would trade in the after-hours session, and that it would move more than $1.00 in the correct direction.

We can extend this reasoning to explain smooth and rapid implied volatility collapse. Suppose, for example, that the $100 strike price options mentioned previously were priced with their characteristic 42% implied volatility at 15:00 with one hour remaining before the final close. An investor who purchased these contracts would be betting on a $1.00 move in the correct direction within 60 minutes. Furthermore, implied volatility would need to plunge to nearly zero over the brief time frame that remained—a discreet move that is completely uncharacteristic for market-priced derivatives. Since we know that implied volatility must fall to nearly zero by the close, and that the chance of a price change of a particular magnitude diminishes at a steady rate, we can predict that implied volatility will collapse smoothly throughout the day. This assertion can be verified using at-the-money option prices and a Black-Scholes calculator.

A more detailed examination reveals that implied volatility collapse has a distinctive profile that can be used to help time entry points for various types of expiration day trades. The fine structure of this profile, which differs between stocks, is apparent in minute-by-minute charts for near-the-money options. In addition, because at-the-money option prices are very sensitive to small changes in the underlying equity price during the final few hours before expiration, implied volatility calculations tend to be noisy. The noise manifests itself as volatility—that is, implied volatility calculations themselves are highly volatile during the final few hours before expiration. Furthermore, irrational behavior among individual traders compounded by relatively low levels of liquidity also contribute to the noise level. This phenomenon is visible in Figure 1.1, which displays expiration day implied volatility profiles for at-the-money put and call options on Goldman Sachs (2008/04/18).

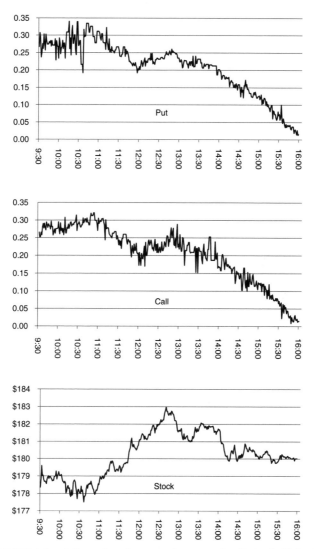

FIGURE 1.1 *Minute-by-minute at-the-money implied volatilities for Goldman Sachs $180 strike price puts (upper chart) and calls (middle chart) on expiration Friday 2008/04/18. Volatility is displayed on the y-axis and time on the x-axis. The lower chart displays minute-by-minute stock prices with price on the y-axis.*

Close scrutiny of the charts reveals that implied volatility becomes more unstable when options are in-the-money. Early in the day, when the stock traded below the $180 strike, put volatilities were highly variable, and call prices were stable. The stock climbed steadily, reaching a peak at 12:41. At this point, the trend reversed; in-the-money $180 call prices became unstable, and out-of-the-money $180 put prices stabilized. These dynamics are directly related to the behavior of traders who are long or short options that suddenly move in-the-money.

For example, consider a trader who sold $180 calls a few days earlier on 4/09 when the option traded for more than $3.00. On expiration day at 10:30 that position could have been closed for a $2.50 profit when the option traded for just $0.50. Unfortunately for this investor, the price climbed 600% to $3.00—the original selling price—when the stock rallied to $183. An aggressive trader protecting substantial profits might have been driven to buy back these options at an aggressive price once the stock crossed the strike price. The trade would have appeared as an upward spike on the implied volatility chart. Exactly when the trade is placed and how aggressive the bidding price is depends on many factors, including size of the position, risk tolerance, view of the market, and experience with the dynamics of expiration day. At the other extreme, a less-aggressive trader with a high tolerance for risk who expected that the stock would return to the strike price might have left the trade open. As it turned out, this approach would have ultimately delivered another $0.45 of profit because the position could have been closed in the final few minutes for just $0.05.

Alternatively, a trader who purchased $180 calls for $0.50 at 10:30 in the morning might have been willing to give up a small amount of profit to quickly close the trade near the peak. The trade would likely have been entered at or below the bidding price. This phenomenon often manifests itself as a long position being closed for less than the amount that the option is in-the-money. The pressure to accept a reduced price for an in-the-money position grows with the size of the trade as liquidity becomes an issue. The result is an instantaneous drop in implied volatility that appears as a downward spike in the chart.

These dynamics complicate the process of building valid and accurate implied volatility profiles. The most straightforward approach is to create a composite profile using out-of-the-money options for each data point in the chart. Figure 1.2 displays the expiration day composite implied volatility profile calculated from the underlying data of Figure 1.1.

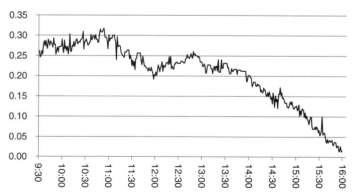

FIGURE 1.2 *Composite implied volatility profile for Goldman Sachs $180 strike price options on expiration Friday 2008/04/18. Implied volatility is displayed on the y-axis, time on the x-axis.*

Finally, these charts display option and stock prices at one-minute intervals. Because stocks are much more liquid than options, it is likely that the final trades for each minute are not precisely aligned in time—that is, the final option trade posted for any given minute is likely to differ from the final stock trade by a few seconds. These small differences can introduce subtle discrepancies in implied volatility if the stock is changing price much faster than the option. We can further improve the quality of the profile, and eliminate these subtle differences, by applying a moving average to smooth the data over a brief time frame of a few minutes. Figure 1.3 displays the same data as Figure 1.2 using a 5-minute moving average.

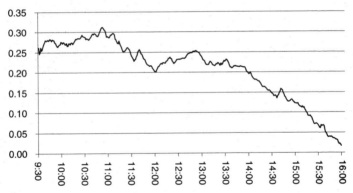

FIGURE 1.3   *Composite implied volatility profile for Goldman Sachs $180 strike price options on expiration Friday 2008/04/18 using a five-minute moving average. Implied volatility is displayed on the y-axis, time on the x-axis.*

The profile reveals distinct intervals that can be used as the basis for structuring trades. The first is characterized by stable or slightly rising implied volatility. It begins at the open and continues until 11:00. At this point, volatility drops quickly from 30% to 20%, where it remains stable until 14:00. The final era of the chart is characterized by a sharp steady decline in implied volatility that continues until the close. Overall there were two stable periods and two periods of rapid decline.

This profile characterizes the expiration day behavior of many heavily traded stocks. Long positions designed to profit from underlying price changes are best structured after implied volatility stabilizes early in the day. These trades benefit from a midday stability window where they suffer time decay but not implied volatility collapse. Conversely, traders who structure early short positions often find that midday price changes can be costly, especially if implied volatility temporarily rises. In the 4/18 Goldman Sachs example, a short at-the-money straddle that sold for $2.26 at 11:44 lost substantial value when the stock climbed to $182.98 at 12:41. The value of the trade climbed to $3.43—a 52% loss. Such mistakes are easy to make because the overwhelming forces on expiration day seem to be implied volatility collapse and attraction to a strike price.

Almost invariably, simple short positions designed to benefit from implied volatility collapse perform best late in the day after the stock stabilizes near a strike price and most large positions have been unwound. These dynamics can be overcome with more complex structures such as ratios and calendar spreads that are hedged against relatively small movements of the underlying stock. This discussion underscores the importance of studying the fine structure of implied volatility.

Implied volatility collapse can become more dramatic when unusual events distort the profile. Earnings releases that immediately precede expiration are the most common example. For example, the April 2008 Google expiration followed an unusual earnings announcement that drove the stock up 90 points. At 14:30, with only 90 minutes remaining before the close, $540 calls traded for $1.30 with the stock at $538.18. The option price reflected elevated levels of implied volatility that persisted after the earnings release. However, from a risk perspective, the price was reasonable because an underlying stock price increase of only $3.12 would have placed these options $1.30 in-the-money. Such an increase was certainly possible since the stock had already climbed $90 from the previous day's close. After rising as high as $542.40, the stock fell back below the strike price to close at $539.85, and the $540 calls were worth just $0.05. The options were surprisingly liquid, with 2,787 contracts changing hands during the final 3 minutes.

A conservative trade that was long $530 calls and short $540 calls delivered outstanding profit because the $530 call that initially traded for $8.50 climbed to $10.00 while the $540 call lost all its value. Furthermore, because the trade had only a 90-minute lifetime and could be closed at any time, an aggressive investor would likely choose to take additional risk by increasing the ratio. If, for example, we structured a trade that was long 10 contracts and short 30 contracts, the opening price would have been $4.60 (long $8.50 – short $3.90). During the final few minutes we would have closed the trade for $9.85 (long $10.00 – short $0.15). Total profit would have been 117% in 90 minutes.

Figure 1.4 depicts the value of the 1:3 ratio trade during its 90-minute lifespan using actual minute-by-minute trading prices for both options. Time of day is measured on the x-axis, and value of the trade on the y-axis.

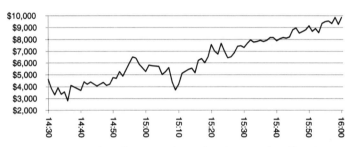

FIGURE 1.4   *Value of a 1:3 ratio trade using Google call options on expiration Friday 2008/04/18. The position was initiated at 14:30 and consisted of 10 long $530 calls and 30 short $540 calls.*

The initial trading price of the $540 calls is surprising because they were $2.00 out-of-the-money with only 90 minutes left before the final close. As always, the correct implied volatility for these contracts can only be calculated using the actual expiration time: Saturday at 23:59. Many option traders mistakenly calculate implied volatility using Friday at 16:00, the time of the final trade, as expiration. Using the Friday close results in a tremendously inflated value of 74% for the $540 call at 14:30. However, if we correctly set expiration at 23:59 the following day, calculated implied volatility takes on a much more reasonable value of 16%. This value is approximately one-half the average implied volatility that was priced into these options during most of the preceding trading month. However, it represents a much more dramatic decline from the implied volatility that was priced into at-the-money Google options the previous evening before earnings were announced (107%). Had it not been expiration day, volatility would likely have stopped falling when it reached traditional levels around 33%. Table 1.1 traces implied volatility for at-the-money calls beginning at the close on Thursday 4/17 and ending at the close on Friday 4/18.

TABLE 1.1   *Implied Volatility History for Google Near-the-Money Call Options Approaching the April 2008 Expiration*

Stock ($)	Date/Time	Option	Trade Price ($)	Implied Volat. (%)
449.88	2008/04/17 16:00	450 call	15.30	106.9
535.21	2008/04/18 09:30	540 call	3.90	42.1
538.18	2008/04/18 14:30	540 call	1.30	15.6
539.85	2008/04/18 16:00	540 call	0.05	0.8

Thursday evening at-the-money $450 calls traded for $15.30 with implied volatility of 107%. During the final minutes of trading on Friday, after the underlying stock climbed $90 to $539.85, at-the-money $540 calls traded for only $0.05, with 0.8% implied volatility. As the table reveals, implied volatility of this option traced a path from 42% at the open to 16% at 14:30 to less than 1% at the close. The profile still exhibited familiar features such as midday stability and late-day accelerated collapse. Figure 1.5 displays the complete profile for $540 puts and calls using the methodology previously described. Once again, the calculations use a 5-minute moving average to smooth out minor inconsistencies.

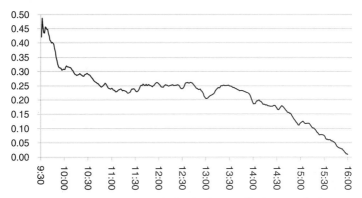

FIGURE 1.5 *Composite implied volatility profile for Google $540 strike price options on expiration Friday 2008/04/18 using a five-minute moving average. Implied volatility is displayed on the y-axis, time on the x-axis.*

I chose this particular example because it illustrates the power of expiration day pricing forces. Despite an earnings announcement that began with 107% implied volatility and ended with a $90 underlying price change, expiration pricing forces dominated, and implied volatility collapsed to 0.8%. That said, trades that rely on implied volatility collapse are not without risk. As always, timing and risk management are important success factors. The downward spike evident in Figure 1.4 at 15:09 represented a temporary positional loss of $0.70 when the stock suddenly spiked to $542.40 and the value of the short side climbed faster than the long side. (The $530 long calls gained $0.20 while the $540 short calls gained $0.30; since the ratio was 1:3, the position lost $0.70.) However, as is common on expiration day, the trade returned to profitability within 2 minutes when the stock fell back to

$541.77. Generally speaking, strike price effects tend to stabilize expiration day positions.

Unfortunately, many option traders expose themselves to unnecessary risk by structuring purely short positions that rely heavily on strike price effects (short straddles being the most common example). Ratio trades are safer because they are hedged against a sudden move of the stock. (Our example was long $530 calls and would have broken even at expiration with the stock trading at $545.) Other structures are certainly possible. We could, for example, have used far-dated options as a hedge by purchasing a calendar spread that was short April $540 calls and long May $540 calls. Structured as a ratio with more short than long contracts, this trade has the same profit potential but different dynamics because of the relatively low delta of the far-dated long options. Throughout this book, we examine various trade structures along with triggers, entry points, and management guidelines.

Strike Price Effects

Strike price effects are an important force in the behavior of all optionable stocks. The most widely recognized effect, "pinning," occurs when a stock hovers very close to a strike price on expiration day. In many cases, the effect can be dramatic, causing the stock to remain within a few cents of a strike price for several hours, sometimes right up to the close. Many market analysts believe that they can predict pinning events many days in advance using a variety of calculations that take into account open interest and distance to nearby strikes. A variety of approaches have evolved; some are quite complex, and most seem to be built on a foundation of solid trading experience. Much of the analysis focuses on the risk to large institutional investors of a stock expiring above or below nearby strike prices. One of the more sophisticated approaches involves analyzing the trading queue to understand whether large trades at a specific strike price tend to be long or short, puts or calls. The underlying assumption is valid because it assumes that the vast majority of very small trades belong to private investors, and that large trades involving hundreds or thousands of contracts are executed by institutional investors. If we assume that institutional investors have more market power, it is easy to see how this analysis could help predict where a stock will ultimately end up on expiration day.

The academic research community has also produced a large body of sophisticated work to document and describe the pinning effect. These papers are all built on a strong statistical foundation of comparisons between optionable and nonoptionable stocks. Setting aside the mathematical complexity, the consensus is that pinning behavior is driven by delta hedging large numbers of long positions. As noted by many active traders, option contracts that exhibit high levels of open interest tend to cause the underlying stock to migrate toward the heavily traded strike price. Pinning and other strike price effects are completely absent in stocks that do not have listed options.

Not surprisingly, these effects are also absent in stocks that have low levels of options open interest or light trading volumes. Stocks that are heavily traded by institutions are the exact opposite—they have high open interest levels and heavy trading volumes. Moreover, on expiration day, each at-the-money contract is likely to change hands many times. It is not uncommon for an option with an open interest of 10,000 contracts to exhibit a trading volume of more than 40,000 contracts on expiration day. This high turnover is a key driving force behind the pinning effect.

Virtually all academic research on the topic has focused on the phenomenon of closing near a strike price on expiration day.[2] However, proximity to a strike price is only a small part of the story. Statistically speaking, the effect is small. For a select group of heavily traded stocks with large open interest, the chance of closing within $0.20 of a strike price during the middle of a trading month is approximately 7%. On expiration Friday, the value nearly doubles to 14%. As we move further from a strike price, the probability must obviously increase. Table 1.2 displays these details for 15 optionable stocks that each have the characteristics described above—heavy trading volumes and large open interest. The data spans 14 expirations from July 2007 to August 2008.

TABLE 1.2   *Number of Expirations within Specific Distances of a Strike Price for 15 Heavily Traded Stocks with Large Options Open Interest (The data spans 14 expirations, 7/2007—8/2008.)*

Ticker	$0.10	$0.20	$0.30	$0.40	$0.50
AAPL	0	1	2	3	4
APA	0	0	0	0	0
DNA	2	4	5	5	5
DVN	0	1	2	2	2
FDX	0	0	0	0	1
GOOG	2	5	6	7	7
GS	3	3	3	4	5
IBM	0	2	3	3	3
LMT	1	1	1	1	2
MA	0	1	2	4	4
MON	1	2	2	3	3
RIG	1	1	1	1	2
RIMM	2	3	3	4	5
SHLD	2	2	4	4	4
X	3	3	4	5	8
Total	17	29	38	46	55

The bottom line of the table displays totals for each distance. We can readily convert these values to percentages by dividing by the total number of possible expiration events. The number of events is equal to 15 stocks × 14 expirations = 210 events. Table 1.3 compares these values to a larger dataset that includes all optionable stocks trading over $50 as well as nonoptionable stocks. The optionable over $50 group includes 392 stocks and, therefore, 5,488 expiration events. The nonoptionable group includes only 100 stocks because most stocks trading for more than $50 are optionable. To ensure valid comparisons, exchange-traded funds and indexes were excluded whether or not they were optionable.

TABLE 1.3   *Percentage of Expirations within Specific Distances of a Strike Price for Three Different Classes of Stocks: Heavily Traded Optionable Stocks Listed in Table 1.2 (Row 1); All Optionable Stocks over $50 (Row 2); and Nonoptionable Stocks over $50 (Row 4) (The third row, included for completeness, displays results for all optionable stocks over $50, with the 15 select stocks of Table 1.2 removed.)*

Group	$0.10	$0.20	$0.30	$0.40	$0.50
15 select stocks (Table 1.2)	8.1%	13.8%	18.1%	21.9%	26.2%
All optionable stocks over $50	5.5%	9.2%	13.7%	17.2%	20.7%
All optionable stocks over $50 (15 select stocks excluded)	5.4%	9.1%	13.5%	17.0%	20.5%
Nonoptionable stocks over $50	6.1%	9.9%	13.7%	16.0%	19.1%

The most striking result displayed in the table is the complete lack of any difference between the broad population of optionable stocks trading above $50 and their nonoptionable counterparts. The stocks originally listed in Table 1.2 (first line of Table 1.3) are clearly more susceptible to pinning on expiration day. The effect is more pronounced when the measurement point is very close to the strike price. Stocks in the select group are approximately 50% more likely to close within $0.10 of a strike price than the larger populations of optionable or nonoptionable stocks. This difference narrows to around 25% when the criterion is widened to a distance of $0.50.

The pinning phenomenon has a strong but complex time component that can be visualized in charts that depict the percentage chance of closing near a strike price as expiration approaches. Institutionally traded stocks display specific characteristics that are absent in the broader population that includes all optionable stocks. Figure 1.6 displays the probability of a stock closing within $0.20 of a strike price on each of the 3 days that precede expiration Friday in addition to the Monday that follows. The final data point, intended as a reference, measures this value 9 trading days (12 calendar days) after expiration. This day was selected for its proximity to the center of the expiration cycle and because it never falls on a weekend or holiday. The solid line profiles the 15 select stocks of Tables 1.2 and 1.3; the dashed line traces the behavior of all optionable stocks over $50.

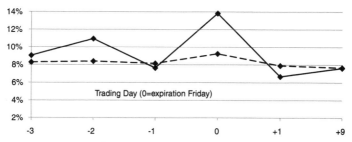

FIGURE 1.6   *Probability of closing within $0.20 of a strike price during the 3 trading days preceding expiration Friday, the first trading day after expiration, and 9 trading days (12 calendar days) after expiration. The dashed line charts data for all optionable stocks over $50, and the solid line charts the 15 select stocks of Table 1.2. The data spans 14 expirations (7/2007—8/2008).[3]*

The shape of the solid line is consistent with a population that responds in complex ways to expiration week pricing dynamics. Its volatile nature reflects the activities of large numbers of traders creating and unwinding positions as the stocks move between strikes. In this regard, it is important to note that expiration week behavior for heavily traded optionable stocks sometimes involves rapid incremental jumps that can move stocks more than their options' implied volatility suggests. This complexity underscores the risks associated with creating positions early in the week that depend on stability in a restricted trading range. Moreover, traditional option pricing models fail under these circumstances, making it difficult to estimate positional risk. Table 1.4 highlights this phenomenon with expiration week price change histories for three stocks that ended the week near a strike price after several surprisingly large price changes.

The three examples were selected from a long list of similar scenarios spanning a timeframe of 14 months. All three stocks closed the week within a few cents of a strike price despite following a highly volatile path. In the first case, Apple Computer touched a low of $165.31 and a high of $182.34—a path that involved 4 strike prices ranging from $165 to $180. The MasterCard example, from an expiration that occurred 7 months earlier, traced a path with a high of $199.50 and a low of $179.50—a 5 strike price scenario spanning the range from $180 to $200. In the third example, Goldman Sachs—April 2008, crossed a midweek low of $161.68, and a high of $183.03 on expiration Friday— 6 strikes were involved. These examples are typical with

TABLE 1.4   Price Change Histories for Three Stocks During Different Expiration Weeks Spanning the Timeframe from November 2007 to June 2008 (In each case, the week's high and low are marked in gray. The closest strikes for each day are noted on the right side of the table.)

Ticker	Date	Weekday	Open	High	Low	Close	Strikes
AAPL	2008/06/13	Fri	171.64	174.16	165.31	172.37	165,170,175
AAPL	2008/06/16	Mon	171.30	177.90	169.07	176.84	170,175,180
AAPL	2008/06/17	Tues	178.10	181.99	177.41	181.43	175,180
AAPL	2008/06/18	Wed	181.12	182.20	177.35	178.75	175,180
AAPL	2008/06/19	Thu	178.55	182.34	176.80	180.90	175,180
AAPL	2008/06/20	Exp Fri	179.35	181.00	175.00	175.27	175,180
MA	2007/11/09	Fri	185.00	199.50	184.00	193.00	185,190,195,200
MA	2007/11/12	Mon	190.83	196.42	180.25	181.88	180,185,190,195
MA	2007/11/13	Tues	183.42	192.23	183.42	188.81	185,190
MA	2007/11/14	Wed	194.23	194.23	186.03	186.77	185,190,195
MA	2007/11/15	Thu	185.00	188.47	182.10	184.88	180,185,190
MA	2007/11/16	Exp Fri	186.00	186.99	179.50	184.87	180,185
GS	2008/04/11	Fri	168.00	171.87	166.87	167.30	165,170
GS	2008/04/14	Mon	166.45	167.55	163.35	163.59	165,170
GS	2008/04/15	Tues	165.06	165.95	161.68	164.20	160,165
GS	2008/04/16	Wed	166.15	169.17	165.91	169.05	165,170
GS	2008/04/17	Thu	167.74	173.50	167.10	172.10	165,170,175
GS	2008/04/18	Exp Fri	176.91	183.03	176.91	179.93	175,180,185

regard to complexity. As is often the case, an investor would have found it difficult to create stable positions early in the week that could be held until expiration without adjustments. No particular trend emerges with regard to rising or falling prices, and the number of strikes involved varies between examples. In some instances, such as the MasterCard example, simple short or long, put or call positions can return very large profits. However, more often than not, these positions result in large interim losses. In both the Apple and Goldman Sachs examples, simple positions composed of a single long or short option would have suffered losses even if the stock ultimately moved in the favorable direction. Generally speaking, directional trades of this sort are tantamount to gambling.

The dashed line of Figure 1.6 can be easily rationalized by calculating the probability of a stock closing within $0.20 of a strike price on any given day. Not surprisingly, that value is very close to 8%. A simple approach is to consider a $100 price range containing 20 strikes spaced by $5.00. The interval we are considering spans $0.40 ($0.20 above and below each strike). Multiplying $0.40 × 20 strikes gives a total area of $8.00 or 8% of the entire $100 space. Another approach involves counting the number of $0.20 intervals in a space equal to half the distance between two strikes. For example, there are 12.5 intervals equal to $0.20 between $100 and $102.50. Each interval, therefore, has an 8% chance of being the final landing point for the stock. In our dataset, which includes optionable stocks over $50, these results may be slightly distorted by $10 strike price spacing for stocks trading above

$200. For these stocks, the probability of landing within $0.20 of a strike price is equal to only 4%. However, only two stocks on the list, Google and MasterCard, fit this description. Google experienced $10 strike spacing across all expirations; MasterCard fell into the $10 spacing category eight times. In total, 22 expiration events had a 4% chance of landing within $0.20 of a strike price, and 188 events fell into the 8% category. Using these values, we can calculate that the probability of a stock on the select list closing within $0.20 of a strike is only slightly affected by $10 spacing—the actual value is 7.6%.

Referring to Table 1.3, we see that all stocks, including those without listed options, have a slightly elevated probability of closing expiration Friday near a strike price. The distortion increases as the interval is decreased. Nonoptionable stocks, for example, close within $0.10 of a strike with a frequency of more than 6%. This value is 2% higher than the random probability—a 50% distortion. Although subtle, these results are statistically significant because they were tabulated across 1,400 expiration events (100 nonoptionable stocks over $50 × 14 expirations). They are also consistent in the sense that the nonoptionable group shows virtually no variability from day to day. This elevated tendency for nonoptionable stocks to close near strike prices undoubtedly represents a slight statistical effect related to buying and selling on $1, $5, and $10 boundaries. Surprisingly, stocks in the nonoptionable group are slightly more likely to close near a strike price than optionable stocks with low institutional trading volume. The small difference is likely related to the final unwinding of large institutional positions near the closing bell, an activity that sometimes causes stocks to drift away from the strike price.

The discussion of strike price effects can be extended in two very specific ways: It can be applied to study pinning behavior on days other than expiration Friday, and it can be modified to measure strike price crosses rather than proximity to a strike price at the closing bell. The second item, strike price crosses, can be used to convincingly demonstrate that heavily traded stocks often display strike price effects throughout the expiration cycle. For example, the 15 stocks listed in Table 1.2 have an 89% chance of crossing a strike price on any given day. This surprisingly high value actually decreases slightly to 82% on expiration Friday when stocks often migrate toward a strike price. The fact that these stocks have approximately a 14% chance of expiring within $0.20 of a strike price may be less relevant than the 82% chance of crossing a strike price. This consistently high probability of trading near a strike price on any given day becomes much more significant on expiration day when the values of at-the-money and out-of-the-money options collapse quickly. For comparison, nonoptionable stocks have approximately a 52% chance of crossing a strike price on any particular day. However, determining a random baseline probability for strike price crosses is a complex problem because the calculation must take into account the underlying volatility of each individual stock.

Exceptionally liquid stocks that have daily volumes in the tens of millions of shares and open interest in the thousands of contracts display very high strike price cross frequencies. Table 1.5 provides relevant details for 5 such stocks during the 14-expiration time frame of Tables 1.2 and 1.3 (7/2007—8/2008). The frequency was determined by counting the number of strike prices that were crossed each day and summing across all expirations. The total for each stock was then divided by the number of expirations (14). In most cases, the frequency of strike price crossings is larger than 1.0 because, on average, more than a single strike was crossed on each day Data for the column labeled "Random Daily Frequency" was recorded in the middle of each expiration cycle, 12 calendar days after expiration Saturday. This day was selected for its proximity to the middle of the month and because it never falls on a holiday.

TABLE 1.5   *Frequency of Strike Price Crosses for Five Heavily Traded Optionable Stocks (Results are calculated for expiration and random days. Column 4 displays the number of closes within $0.20 of a strike price summed across 14 expirations.)*

Ticker	Expiration Day Frequency	Random Daily Frequency	$0.20 Pinning, 14 Expirations
AAPL	1.07	1.14	1
GOOG	1.29	1.29	5
GS	1.14	0.93	3
MA	0.93	1.43	1
RIMM	1.00	0.79	3

The high values displayed in the table, both for expiration and random days, underscore the power of the strike price effect. Three of the stocks—Apple, Google, and MasterCard—averaged more than one strike price cross on a typical day. Goldman Sachs and Research in

Motion were less likely to cross a strike on a random day, but averaged at least a single cross on each expiration day. Only one of the five stocks, MasterCard, experienced a significant drop in frequency on expiration day. Google crossed the same number of strikes on the 14 expiration days as on the 14 random days (18 strikes/14 expirations). Two of the five stocks, Apple and MasterCard, exhibited reduced strike cross frequencies on expiration day. This behavior is consistent with reduced pinning levels—each closed within $0.20 of a strike only 1 time in 14 expirations.

Stocks such as Apple and MasterCard that often fail to close near a strike price but have very high strike cross frequencies are excellent candidates for certain types of expiration day trades such as long straddles. The key to trading each of these stocks lies in understanding their minute-by-minute expiration day behavior. Although they may exhibit similar characteristics with regard to the probability of closing near a strike price, stocks that tend to decouple from a strike near the close are distinctly different from stocks that rarely pin to a strike at all. Because daily data is too coarse for this analysis, we use minute-by-minute data to build trading models throughout this book.

The contrast between daily and minute-by-minute data can be surprising. For example, the daily strike cross frequencies listed in Table 1.5, although very high, are understated with respect to minute-by-minute frequencies. In this regard, the daily frequency for Apple Computer reveals that the stock crosses a strike price, on average, at least once each day. However, the minute-by-minute data reveals that Apple has more than a 5% chance of crossing a strike price during any particular minute, which translates into 20 crosses per day. How these 20 crosses are distributed is key to understanding the behavior of the stock—especially on expiration day. Extending Table 1.5 with minute-by-minute data reveals surprisingly high strike price cross frequencies for all five stocks. These values could not have been predicted from the daily information. Table 1.6 contains the extensions calculated as the probability of crossing a strike price during each minute of a typical trading day. The information was obtained by counting the number of minutes containing a strike price cross during an entire trading year (approximately 98,132 minutes).[4]

These probabilities can rise or fall sharply on expiration day depending on the behavior of the stock near strike prices. Table 1.7 illustrates this concept by comparing the behavior of one stock, Research in Motion, on two different expiration days.

The March expiration, strongly characterized by pinning, ended with the stock just $0.06 out-of-the-money. The July expiration was much different because the stock closed directly centered between two strikes. However, on both days the stock crossed two strikes. The difference was revealed in minute-by-minute data, which counted 40 strike price crosses on the day where pinning was strongly evident and only 9 crosses on the nonpinning day. The probability of crossing a strike price boundary during a single minute of the March expiration was nearly five times higher than during the July expiration.

TABLE 1.6   Strike Price Cross Frequencies for Five Stocks in Different Time Frames (Columns 2 and 3 display daily frequencies; column 4 lists probabilities calculated across an entire trading year by counting the number of minutes that contain a strike price cross.)

Tickers	Expiration Day Frequency	Random Daily Frequency	Single-Minute Probability	$0.20 Pinning, 14 Expirations
AAPL	1.07	1.14	5.5%	1
GOOG	1.29	1.29	7.3%	5
GS	1.14	0.93	5.9%	3
MA	0.93	1.43	5.7%	1
RIMM	1.00	0.79	4.8%	3

TABLE 1.7   Price Change Behavior for Research in Motion Described in Terms of Strike Price Crosses on Two Different Expiration Dates

Expiration Date	High ($)	Low ($)	Close ($)	Strikes Crossed	Num. of Crosses	Probability (Minute)	Closing Distance
2008/03/20	106.14	99.70	104.94	2	40	10.3%	$0.06
2008/07/18	115.26	107.06	112.85	2	9	2.3%	$2.15

Finally, a rarely mentioned result of pinning is the tendency of some stocks to exhibit unusually large price changes on the Monday following expiration. This tendency can be exploited by purchasing long straddles just a few minutes before expiration on stocks that close expiration Friday pinned to a strike price. Statistically speaking, these straddles generate disproportionately large returns because they are mispriced.

Time Decay

Time decay is the overriding dynamic that characterizes the final days before expiration. The percentage of time lost between trading sessions dramatically accelerates as expiration approaches because the options market is open for 6.5 hours each day and closed for 17.5 hours. The magnitude of the decline traces a path that has two significant peaks: the weekend preceding expiration, and the final evening. During the weekend that precedes expiration, an option contract loses 32.8% of its remaining time. Thursday evening before the final trading day, 31.3% of the remaining time disappears. The percentage of remaining time lost between trading sessions is displayed in Figure 1.7.

Applying these parameters to the value of an at-the-money straddle reveals significant distortions that would normally cause the position to be overpriced each evening. Figure 1.8 profiles these changes for a $100 straddle priced with 50% implied volatility and 1.5% risk-free interest, beginning on the Friday that precedes expiration week. Each pair of points on the curve represents daily opening and closing prices for the straddle.

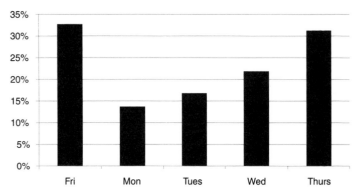

FIGURE 1.7   *Percentage of time lost between trading sessions in the days leading up to expiration.*

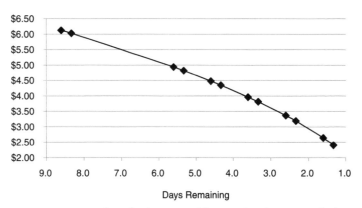

FIGURE 1.8   *Value of a $100 straddle priced with 50% implied volatility and 1.5% risk free interest beginning on the Friday preceding expiration week. Each pair of points on the curve represents daily opening and closing prices for the straddle.*

Note that the number of days remaining is calculated with expiration set as Saturday evening at 23:59. The chart uses precise values that range from 8.603 at the open on Friday to 1.333 days at the final close. Because we are using constant implied volatility of 50%, the straddle is still valued at $2.41 at the final close on expiration Friday. This value would represent tremendous overpricing of the position because the options cannot be traded after the close. As we have seen, the market responds to this distortion with a sharp implied volatility collapse on the final day. This collapse is the last and largest of the week, which also includes daily implied volatility swings. Each evening as the closing bell draws near, implied volatility decreases, and bid-ask spreads widen in response to the impending overnight time decay. By the final evening, however, the distortion is large enough that it cannot be covered. As a result, at-the-money and near-the-money options typically lose nearly one-third of their value when the market opens on expiration Friday. Therefore, properly structured short positions and ratios have the potential to deliver very large returns. Table 1.8 outlines appropriate implied volatility adjustments that are required to compensate for intersession time decay each evening. The implied volatility priced into each day's close is precisely set so that returning to 50% implied volatility at the next open will not change the position value.

TABLE 1.8   *Implied Volatility Adjustments Designed to Compensate for Intersession Time Decay (Pricing is for a $100 straddle with 50% implied volatility and a 1.5% risk-free interest rate.)*

Day	Time	Implied Volat.	Price	Change
Fri	9:30	50.0%	$6.12	
Fri	16:00	41.0%	$4.94	19.3%
Mon	9:30	50.0%	$4.94	
Mon	16:00	46.5%	$4.48	9.3%
Tue	9:30	50.0%	$4.48	
Tue	16:00	45.6%	$3.96	11.6%
Wed	9:30	50.0%	$3.96	
Wed	16:00	44.2%	$3.37	14.9%
Thu	9:30	50.0%	$3.37	
Thu	16:00	41.5%	$2.64	21.7%
Fri	9:30	50.0%	$2.64	

Investors can capitalize on the market's adjustment to overnight time decay without suffering the risks of overnight exposure by creating short positions in the morning and closing them at the end of the trading session. This strategy provides its greatest advantage on the Friday preceding expiration week when the compensating price change is more than 19%. However, the market response is generally not 100% efficient, and the full amount of intersession loss is often not realized unless the trade is left on until the next open.

Table 1.9 illustrates these dynamics using the August 2008 Goldman Sachs expiration. The table traces the trading price and implied volatility for the $175 call from the open on Friday 8/8 through the close on Monday 8/11.

TABLE 1.9 *Goldman Sachs $175 Call Trading Price and Implied Volatility Friday 2008/08/08 through Monday 2008/08/11*

Date/Time	Days Remaining	Stock Price ($)	175 Call Price ($)	Implied Volatility
2008/08/08 9:31	8.60	173.27	3.40	39.2%
2008/08/08 16:00	8.33	175.64	4.00	34.4%
2008/08/11 9:31	5.60	176.41	4.45	42.4%
2008/08/11 16:00	5.33	176.89	4.55	41.3%

The real-life implied volatility picture is slightly more complex than the theoretical description. In addition to the anticipated decline, values were slightly depressed throughout the trading day on the Friday preceding expiration. At-the-money $175 calls opened the day at 39.2% and declined to 34.4% at the close. After the weekend, the option price reflected 42.4% implied volatility in the very first trading minute (approximately 3 percentage points higher than the previous week's average). We know that these slight anomalies were not the result of overall market volatility swings because the VIX traded just above 20 throughout both sessions. However, Goldman Sachs was quite active during expiration week. It opened the Monday session at $176.38 and climbed as high as $183.20 but closed the week trading at only $163.18. The details are relevant to option traders seeking to construct expiration week strategies.

Sample Trade Structures

In the chapters that follow, we review a small list of focused trading strategies that capitalize on the three dynamics mentioned earlier: volatility collapse, pinning, and time decay. The trades have surprisingly different risk/return profiles.

Table 1.10 outlines an overnight ratio trade that takes advantage of the time decay distortion of the final evening before expiration. The first pair of entries represents the initial trade that is long 10 contracts of $120 calls and short 30 contracts of $125 calls for a stock trading at $123. The second pair contains prices for the same trade at 10:00 the following morning. The stock price has not changed, and implied volatility has declined slightly from 42% to 36%. The trade generates a 95% profit.

The protective value of the long $120 calls is evident in the second table (Table 1.11), which reveals results for the trade if the stock climbs $2.00 before the open on Friday. Despite the run-up, the trade still generates substantial profit (52%). Furthermore, if the stock appears to be pinned to the $125 strike, the trade should be held until the market close because all value will disappear from the short $125 calls. Under these circumstances the trade will generate another $3,570 of profit (closing the trade at 4:00 will net nearly $5,000 and a total profit of 400%).

TABLE 1.10 *Sample Overnight Ratio Trade That Leverages Time Decay Distortion of the Final Evening before Expiration*

Position	Date/Time	Stock Price ($)	Call Price ($)	Contracts	Position Value ($)	Total ($)
Short $125 call	2008/04/17 16:00	123	0.86	-30.00	-2,580	
Long $120 call	2008/04/17 16:00	123	3.56	10.00	3,560	980
Short $125 call	2008/04/18 10:00	123	0.44	-30.00	-1,320	
Long $120 call	2008/04/18 10:00	123	3.23	10.00	3,230	1,910

TABLE 1.11 *Sample Overnight Ratio Trade with $2.00 Underlying Price Increase*

Position	Date/Time	Stock Price ($)	Call Price ($)	Contracts	Position Value ($)	Total ($)
Short $125 call	2008/04/17 16:00	123	0.86	-30.00	-2,580	
Long $120 call	2008/04/17 16:00	123	3.56	10.00	3,560	980
Short $125 call	2008/04/18 10:00	125	1.19	-30.00	-3,570	
Long $120 call	2008/04/18 10:00	125	5.06	10.00	5,060	1,490

This scenario represents the norm rather than the exception on expiration day because migration to a strike price combined with implied volatility collapse and accelerated time decay are the dominant forces. The final version of the example is outlined in the following table for completeness. Table 1.12 displays the Thursday evening initial position, Friday morning interim profit point, and Friday closing prices.

Our brief outline of this trade would not be complete without mentioning the downside risk. If the stock price had declined sharply overnight and both sides of the trade collapsed to zero, we would have lost our initial investment, $980. However, this scenario is very unlikely on expiration day. Furthermore, if the stock opened down 10%, the long side would still retain approximately half its value, and we would close the trade Friday morning with just a $400 loss. The risk/return profile is very favorable when the forces of expiration day are fully considered. Generally speaking, the risk of such a trade lies on the upside because the stock can rally beyond the upper strike price and the point where the long hedge is effective. Our discussion includes a detailed analysis of these risks along with guidelines for selecting trade candidates.

TABLE 1.12 *Completed Sample Overnight Ratio Trade with $2.00 Underlying Price Increase*

Position	Date/Time	Stock Price ($)	Call Price ($)	Contracts	Position Value ($)	Total ($)
Short $125 call	2008/04/17 16:00	123	0.86	–30.00	–2,580	
Long $120 call	2008/04/17 16:00	123	3.56	10.00	3,560	980
Short $125 call	2008/04/18 10:00	125	1.19	–30.00	–3,570	
Long $120 call	2008/04/18 10:00	125	5.06	10.00	5,060	1,490
Short $125 call	2008/04/18 16:00	125	0.05	–30.00	–150	
Long $120 call	2008/04/18 16:00	125	5.00	10.00	5,000	4,850

Conservative investors also have the option of avoiding all overnight exposure by only structuring trades on expiration Friday after the market opens. I have personally taken this approach in my own trading because the profit potential is enormous and the risk is limited to very moderate time decay that can be eliminated at any time by closing a trade. The simplest and most effective strategy is based on purchasing long straddles on stocks with a history of large expiration day price changes. The trade is normally executed at a point of symmetry when the stock crosses a strike price during the midday flat implied volatility window. In this scenario, it is common for a $2.00 long straddle to generate profits of more than 300%. Our earlier example mentioned near the beginning of this chapter involving the Oil Service HOLDRS Trust (OIH) was modest by expiration day standards. During the previous expiration (March 2008), Goldman Sachs climbed from $166 to $180, and MasterCard from $204 to $220. Although each stock eventually pinned to a strike price, long positions purchased near the open generated returns in the neighborhood of 1,000% (10×).

Many different trade structures were possible, including the purchase of out-of-the-money options that traded for $0.30 at the open and $10 at the close. Consider, for example, the concept of risking just a few hundred dollars on 10 contracts of Goldman Sachs $170 calls that traded near $0.30 at the open and $10 at the close. Furthermore, a variety of indicators, including open interest and option volume, at various strikes strongly hinted that this scenario would play out. By 10:50 the trend was clear—the stock decoupled from the $170 strike where it had been trading for approximately 30 minutes and rapidly climbed $4.00. A conservative investor could have purchased a $170 straddle at 10:50 and closed the trade 1 hour later with approximately 300% profit. That same investor would likely have found other trading opportunities before 2:00 when the stock began its final rapid ascent from $174 to $180.

Summary

Exploiting expiration-related price distortions is an excellent way to generate profit without suffering the risks associated with constant exposure to the equity markets. More significantly, the strategies outlined in these pages do not depend on predicting the direction that a stock will move. Readers will notice that the discussions lack traditional charts and associated indicators, such as moving averages, stochastics, support and resistance levels, and so on. There are many fine books and excellent websites devoted to technical charting, and readers are encouraged to experiment with applications that combine technical charting with expiration pricing dynamics.

The examples chosen for this discussion were intentionally selected from recent expirations at the time of this writing. However, the forces responsible for expiration day behavior have persisted for many years through bull and bear markets, and they will continue into the distant future. Wild, unpredictable markets provide additional advantages for expiration day traders who understand the dynamics and can take advantage of the large swings with well-structured long positions. This dynamic became strongly evident during the 30% market collapse that occurred during September and October 2008. Implied volatility climbed above 100% for many heavily traded options. In such scenarios, expiration week swings are enormous, and the implied volatility collapse on the final day can generate surprisingly large profits in just a couple of hours. Ratio trades that are hedged against modest price changes are particularly effective in this environment, and it is sometimes possible to move beyond the nearest strike price for the short side of the trade.

Endnotes

1. Equity and index options actually expire on Saturday at 11:59 EST, but the final trading moment for a public customer is Friday at 4:00. In-the-money options are typically traded to a broker during the final few minutes when all time value has run out. The broker exercises the options by calling or putting the stock at the contract price. Index options are often exercised into cash because the underlying security does not trade.

2. Strike prices are normally set at the following intervals: $2.50 when the strike price is $25 or less; $5.00 when the strike price is between $25 and $200; and $10.00 for strikes over $200. At the time of this writing, the Chicago Board Options Exchange was experimenting with $1.00 spacing for stocks up to $50 and $2.50 strike spacing for stocks up to $75.

3. The chart includes minor adjustments for three market holidays: Monday 2008/01/21, Monday 2008/02/18, and Friday 2008/03/21. In each case, the adjustment shifts the count forward or back one trading day, as appropriate. Because Friday 2008/03/21 was a holiday, day 0 was Thursday 2008/03/20.

4. The data for these calculations was carefully screened to ensure that none of the trades occurred during pre- or postmarket sessions.

Chapter 2

Working with Statistical Models

Different Populations

As we saw in Chapter 1, "Expiration Pricing Dynamics," the key dynamics that make expiration unique are closely linked to the trading characteristics of individual stocks. Nonoptionable stocks and optionable stocks with low open interest levels both lack strike price effects. These effects are most often associated with equities that are heavily traded by institutional investors. The activities of these traders involve initiating and unwinding substantial stock and option positions that are highly sensitive to small moves in- or out-of-the-money. These situations, which tend to be self-canceling, cause stocks to trade near a strike price. The effects are enhanced on expiration day by knowledgeable traders who recognize the effect and place sell orders just above a strike price and buy orders just below.

This book describes a very specific type of day trading that depends on understanding the price change behavior of individual stocks during the days preceding expiration. It requires an unusual blend of option trading skills and statistical insight. Most important of all, however, is the recognition that the analysis must be stock specific. In this regard, our discussion diverges from those of the academic literature that tends to focus on the behavior of all optionable stocks as a group.

In the preceding chapter, we saw that the statistics for a set of 15 optionable stocks with heavy trading volumes and large open interest were significantly different from the broader population of all optionable stocks. Whereas the broad population had only a slightly elevated chance of closing expiration day within $0.20 of a strike price, the select group was 73% more likely than could be expected from a random distribution. Applying this analysis to five specific members of the group—Apple Computer (AAPL), Google (GOOG), Goldman Sachs (GS), MasterCard (MA), Research in Motion (RIMM)—raises the increase to 125%. Furthermore, if we measure the number of strike price crossings across all the groups, we find that the number is dramatically higher for the group of five; more than one crossing per day at any random point in the expiration cycle. This behavior is precisely what we are attempting to exploit on expiration day when the value of at-the-money options collapses in exponential decay. Whether or not a stock expires very close to a strike price is not nearly as important as its behavior throughout the day. We are seeking stocks that have a history of migrating to a strike, hovering near a strike, or decoupling from a strike and jumping to the next or beyond. These opportunities are the ones most likely to generate large amounts of profit.

Table 2.1 summarizes these statistics for the 3 populations previously mentioned—optionable stocks over $50, 15 select stocks mentioned in the preceding chapter, and the 5 very heavily traded stocks listed above. As in the previous chapter, "random day" refers to a day in the middle of each expiration cycle, 12 calendar days after expiration Saturday. This particular day was selected for its proximity to the middle of the month and because it never falls on a holiday.

TABLE 2.1   *Summary Statistics for Three Populations (The first two columns contrast the probability of closing within $0.20 of a strike price on expiration day and on a random day. The last two columns display the probability of crossing a strike price on expiration day and on a random day.)*

	Expir. Day < $0.20	Random Day < $0.20	Expir. Day Crosses	Random Day Crosses
Optionable Stocks > $50	9.2%	7.7%	49.0%	48.3%
15 select stocks	13.8%	7.6%	82.4%	88.6%
5 select stocks	18.6%	7.1%	108.6%	111.4%

The data underscores the importance of focusing on price change behavior for individual stocks and very small, precisely defined populations. A couple of significant differences emerge. The carefully selected group of five stocks exhibits very high strike crossing frequencies—more than twice that of the broad population consisting of all optionable stocks over $50. On expiration day, the same stocks also close very near a strike price more than twice as often as the general population, and 35% more often than the select group of 15 stocks.

We can capitalize on these population-specific behavioral characteristics using several different strategies. For example, we can structure short positions that capitalize on implied volatility collapse and pinning for small groups of stocks like the five listed earlier. Such trades are not restricted to this group because many stocks tend to hover near a strike price on expiration day before drifting away during the final few minutes. A disciplined approach that closes each trade according to carefully selected parameters has the same profit potential for any stock that trades near a strike price on expiration day. Moreover, expiration day trading is a very active process that involves opening and closing positions many times in just a few hours. These dynamics are true for all trades regardless of the stocks selected. The process sometimes involves different approaches at different times of the day. For example, an investor might buy a long straddle during the middle of the day when implied volatility is stable, wait for a large price change, close the position, and open a new short trade when the same stock settles near a strike price. This trade might then be closed and reopened several times as the stock drifts away from and returns to the strike price. Following this approach significantly increases the number of possible stock choices.

It is also possible to exploit expiration dynamics to profit from short positions at distant strike prices. A few years ago with the VIX hovering near 10, implied volatilities were generally too low to exploit distant strike prices in the final hours before expiration. However, in the fourth quarter of 2008, the VIX rose sharply, often closing above 70. This situation raised implied volatility for many active stocks to unprecedented levels above 150%. Many of these stocks previously had options trading for 30% to 40%.

Throughout this book, we explore different types of expiration week behavior with the goal of identifying appropriate trades for different scenarios. For consistency, our discussion tends to focus on the five stocks listed earlier. Many different pieces of data, including minute-by-minute pricing and volume information for both the stock and relevant options, are required to assemble complete and accurate scenarios. This information is invaluable because it drives the calculation of implied and actual volatilities and allows precise comparisons of structured positions. Expiration trading strategies rely on price distortions that are best understood at the individual stock level. In this regard, it makes more sense to thoroughly study individual stocks in great detail than to gain an overview of a large population. Each trade has the potential to deliver tremendous profit, and because day trading is the focus, it is difficult to manage many simultaneous positions. In keeping with this theme, our discussion focuses on detail at the individual stock level.

Selecting Candidates

The preceding chapter outlined a general profile for implied volatility collapse on expiration day. This profile can be used to help time entry points for specific types of trades. The next step is to select candidates. The most thorough approach involves analyzing historical data on individual stocks and using this information to make trading decisions. However, an astute trader can accomplish this task by watching several stocks on expiration day and noting their behavior. Stocks that tend to cross a strike and continue moving into the interstrike zone are excellent candidates for long straddles. Conversely, stocks that hover close to strike prices are better candidates for short positions that benefit from implied volatility collapse and time decay.

Traditional metrics such as pinning are poor measures of such behavior because it matters little whether a stock closes the day within a specific distance of a strike price. Goldman Sachs, for example, closed the March 2008 expiration within $0.37 of a strike price at $179.63 after crossing a total of three strikes: $170, $175, and $180. Stocks that frequently exhibit this sort of behavior will easily be mistaken as candidates for short positions when, in reality, they are long straddle candidates.

Stocks that move away from a strike and return are also difficult to trade using short positions if the magnitude of the move is large enough to cause a significant interim loss for the trade. Furthermore, once a stock moves a significant distance into the interstrike zone, normal trading forces are likely to drive the stock to the next strike price. We, therefore, need a metric that distinguishes between stocks that tend to close near a strike after erratic behavior and stocks with more predictable trading characteristics.

Table 2.2 compares the five stocks on our list using two simple measurements: the number of minutes that contain a strike price cross, and the number of minutes where the stock traded more than $1 from a strike price.[1] The $1 parameter was chosen with actual trading dynamics in mind. In virtually all cases, a long straddle opened when a stock crosses a strike will deliver significant profit when one side of the trade is $1 in-the-money. The very best candidates for such trades are stocks that frequently cross a strike price where a neutral trade can be placed but also tend to move far into the interstrike zone where at-the-money straddles become profitable. Dividing the number of $1 in-the-money minutes by the number of strike cross minutes gives a ratio that can be directly used for this comparison. The data spans 12 expirations from September 2007 through August 2008.

TABLE 2.2   *Summary Data for 5 Stocks (12 Expirations) Comparing the Number of Minutes That Contain a Strike Price Cross to the Number of Minutes Where Each Stock Traded More Than $1 from a Strike (The final column lists the number of expirations within $0.30 of a strike.)*

Ticker	Minutes > $1 from Strike	Strike Crosses	Ratio	Expirations < $0.30 from Strike
AAPL	2,847	147	19.37	2
GOOG	2,740	498	5.50	4
GS	2,845	285	9.98	2
MA	3,100	306	10.13	1
RIMM	1,952	223	8.75	3

The ratio of in-the-money minutes to strike cross minutes is very descriptive. For example, the data reveals that during any given expiration day minute, Apple Computer (AAPL) is 19 times more likely to trade at least $1 in-the-money than to cross a strike price. Google (GOOG), however, exhibits a much lower ratio of only 5.5. Statistically speaking, an investor who sold straddles on both would discover that Apple trades were much more difficult to manage than Google trades. Conversely, long straddles on Apple were much more likely to return a profit.

The rightmost column displays the number of expirations within $0.30 of a strike price for each stock. This column represents a traditional measure of pinning. The numbers are misleading because Apple, the least stable member of the group, displays approximately the same pinning behavior as the other stocks. As always, details are important. Consider, for example, a comparison with MasterCard (MA), which exceeds Apple with regard to the number of minutes outside the $1 threshold but maintains a much lower overall ratio (10.13) of out-of-the-money to at-the-money minutes. The reason is related to the high number of strike crosses which make up the denominator of the ratio. Apple crossed a strike price only 147 times during the 12 expirations tracked, whereas MasterCard crossed 306 times. In addition, MasterCard expired within $0.30 of a strike only once in 12 months. These dynamics make MasterCard a terrific long straddle candidate. In percentage terms, 6.6% of expiration day minutes involved a strike cross for MasterCard, while Apple touched a strike price just 3.1% of the time. Despite its higher strike cross frequency, MasterCard still traded more than $1 from a strike 66% of the time (the number for Apple was 61%).[2] In practical trading terms, MasterCard offered many more entry points for long straddles.

We can extend this analysis with summary data that includes information for each stock on each expiration date. This level of detail enables us to reach beyond generalizations by matching specific situations to market conditions. We know, for example, that 4 of the 12 expirations occurred during earnings seasons. The effects can be significant when a company releases its quarterly results just before the final trading day. For example, Goldman Sachs announced earnings on 2008/03/18, just 2 days before expiration. The results were shocking. After declining more than 27% in 4 months, a surprisingly positive report from Goldman Sachs gave the Dow its largest point gain in more than 5 years and rallied the stock 16%. The result two days later was an expiration that crossed 3 strike prices and moved the stock nearly 8%. This particular time frame was remarkable for its rising volatility and large market swings, which were driven by turbulence in the banking industry caused by catastrophic subprime lending losses. Bear Stearns, the first major casualty, was acquired in an emergency government-funded bailout just the day before Goldman Sachs released its earnings. That event caused Goldman to fall from a high of $167.80 on Friday 3/14 to a low of $140.27 on Monday after the Bear Stearns problem was announced.

Other significant financial events included a 2.1% decline in the Dow and a 3.5% drop in the Hang Seng Index the day before expiration—all related to problems in the financial sector.

This sort of information can be used as a supplement to the underlying statistical data to make intelligent expiration day trading decisions. If we trace the behavior of Goldman Sachs during the days leading up to expiration, we see that the stock crossed many strike prices in its fall from the high 160s to the low 140s before rebounding to open above $166 on expiration day. In all, the stock visited 6 strike prices on the way down, and the same 6 strikes on the way back up. This situation wreaked havoc among both institutional and private investors who were forced to unwind and reset complex positions several times in only a few days. A shrewd options trader who recognized the instability could have capitalized on these dynamics by purchasing straddles at the right time on expiration day. Conversely, an investor who knew something about strike price effects and counted on pinning might have made a serious mistake by launching a short position when the stock appeared to "pin" to the $170 strike at 10:00. Figure 2.1 displays the false pinning behavior displayed by the stock between 10:00 and 10:30 on March 20 using minute-by-minute closing prices.

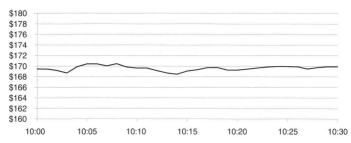

FIGURE 2.1 *False pinning of Goldman Sachs stock to the $170 strike on expiration day—March 20, 2008. The stock ultimately climbed above both the $175 and $180 strikes before closing at $179.63. Time is measured on the x-axis, price on the y-axis.*

Tables 2.3 through 2.7 contain detailed summaries for each of the 5 stocks across 12 expirations. Each table includes an additional column containing information about the high and low for the day. This column, labeled (H − L) / C, calculates the magnitude of the high-low span as a percentage of the closing price. In the Goldman Sachs example discussed previously, the stock traversed a range equal to nearly 8% of its closing price. As revealed in the table, this value is approximately twice that of a normal expiration day. The September 2007 expiration represented a similar opportunity. After quarterly earnings were released the previous day, the stock climbed $5 from its open at $205.56 to its close at $209.98. Although the table accurately lists only one strike as being crossed (the trading price briefly climbed above $210), the stock actually traversed a distance equal to the distance between two strikes. As is often the case, pinning was a misleading measure of the stock's behavior, which was much more volatile than the at-the-money expiration would indicate. The ratio of minutes that traded more than $1 from a strike to minutes containing a strike cross reveals much more about the path taken by the stock. The value was more than double (20.1) the average (9.98) for the one-year time frame.

Like Goldman Sachs, Google often announces earnings very close to expiration. In the case of Goldman, however, not all earnings announcements immediately preceded the final trading day, as noted in the heading for Table 2.3. In March 2008, the final trading day was 3/20, and earnings were announced before the opening bell on 3/18—a gap of 2 days before the final open of the expiration cycle. December 2007 and June 2008 had three-day gaps. All four Goldman Sachs earnings announcements were made before the market opened. Conversely, each of the three shaded expirations for Google followed a quarterly earnings announcement made after the previous day's closing bell. Each event triggered large trading volumes and substantial price changes in the after- and premarket sessions preceding the final session.

TABLE 2.3 Goldman Sachs, Summary Data for 12 Expirations (The March 20 and September 21 expirations discussed earlier are shaded gray, as are the other expirations that closely followed a quarterly earnings announcement. The first shaded expiration, September 2007, was unique because earnings were announced before the open on the previous day. Each of the other three expirations followed a brief gap, as follows: 12/21—3 days; 3/20—2 days; 6/20—3 days.)

Date	>$1 from Strike	Total Crosses	(H − L) / C	Strikes Crossed	Closing Distance to Strike ($)	Open ($)	Close ($)
2007/09/21	341	17	0.033	1	-0.02	205.56	209.98
2007/10/19	233	35	0.045	1	-2.31	226.15	217.69
2007/11/16	377	0	0.031	0	-4.75	228.26	225.25
2007/12/21	127	40	0.025	1	-0.40	205.85	209.60
2008/01/18	268	19	0.047	2	2.21	192.17	187.21
2008/02/15	146	16	0.030	1	-1.59	175.10	178.41
2008/03/20	233	19	0.079	3	-0.37	166.30	179.63
2008/04/18	187	38	0.034	1	-0.07	176.91	179.93
2008/05/16	388	0	0.019	0	2.14	189.55	187.14
2008/06/20	65	71	0.021	1	-1.23	185.02	183.77
2008/07/18	263	24	0.030	1	-2.16	183.08	182.84
2008/08/15	217	6	0.033	1	-1.82	167.40	163.18
Average (abs)			0.036		1.59		
Total	2,845	285					
Ratio	9.98						

During the year profiled in Table 2.4, the company released its quarterly report immediately after the previous evening's close three times. Each of these events is shaded gray. The October 2007 expiration closed nearly $5 in-the-money, and the other two expirations—April and July 2008—each crossed two different strike prices. High-low values for both days were surprisingly high, at 4.3% of the closing price. In April, the stock fell as low as $524.77 and climbed as high as $547.70; the July values were $478.19 and $498.98, respectively. Although high and low prices are not listed in the tables, the (H – L) / C ratio can be used to accurately calculate the magnitude of the price change. For April, the value is given by 4.3% × 539.41; for July it is 4.3% × 481.32. April's number is particularly surprising because the stock closed only $4.20 above its opening price after tracing a path that spanned $23. In this context, it is important to remember that options on stocks above $200 have $10 strike spacing. Ignoring this distinction has caused statistical distortions in several academic research papers about pinning.

TABLE 2.4 Google Summary Data for 12 Expirations (Three expirations that immediately followed an earnings release are shaded gray. In each case, quarterly results were announced after the close of the market the evening before expiration Friday. The January 2008 results were announced 13 days after expiration Friday.)

Date	> $1 from Strike	Total Crosses	(H − L) / C	Strikes Crossed	Closing Distance to Strike ($)	Open ($)	Close ($)
2007/09/21	79	59	0.014	1	0.10	556.34	560.10
2007/10/19	151	63	0.024	1	4.71	654.56	644.71
2007/11/16	186	82	0.031	2	3.63	633.94	633.63
2007/12/21	380	0	0.009	0	−3.31	697.88	696.69
2008/01/18	306	4	0.019	1	0.25	608.36	600.25
2008/02/15	270	37	0.016	1	−0.36	528.31	529.64
2008/03/20	249	48	0.042	2	3.55	427.32	433.55
2008/04/18	225	44	0.043	2	−0.59	535.21	539.41
2008/05/16	90	80	0.011	1	0.07	581.43	580.07
2008/06/20	251	29	0.023	1	−3.57	556.98	546.43
2008/07/18	255	31	0.043	2	1.32	498.35	481.32
2008/08/15	298	21	0.010	1	0.15	506.99	510.15
Average (abs)			0.024		1.80		
Total	2,740	498					
Ratio	5.50						

Google is the best example in the group of a stock that displays true pinning effects. Despite $10 strike spacing, the stock averages a close to strike distance of only $1.80. This distance is equal to 0.3% of the average closing price during the time frame of our analysis. Surprisingly, the pinning behavior tends to transcend highly active days that follow an earnings report. October 2007 was the exception because the stock closed near the midpoint of two strikes: $640 and $650. The two other earnings-influenced expirations listed in the table each experienced much larger high to low price changes (4.3%) while still closing closer to a strike. Particularly interesting was the April 2008 expiration because the stock opened more than $85 above its previous close and ultimately climbed another $4. Despite tremendous moves that involved crossing nine strikes and closing near the tenth, the final trade was just $0.59 out-of-the-money. Moreover, minute-by-minute analysis reveals that the stock pinned tightly to the $540 strike during the final 30 minutes of trading. Between 15:30 and 16:00 the price varied only a few cents above and below the $540 strike. Furthermore, high implied volatility that persisted after the earnings release made short positions particularly profitable. Specifically, ratios that were long $530 calls and short $540 calls delivered outstanding profit, as did short $540 straddles. Finally, the high percentage chance of the stock crossing a strike during any particular minute coupled with a small (High − Low) / Close ratio is consistent with pinning behavior. Broadly speaking, Google is an excellent candidate for short positions on expiration day.

TABLE 2.5 *Apple Computer, Summary Data for 12 Expirations (Earnings events are not marked because they occurred after options expiration. Quarterly earnings were not released before any of the expirations in the table.)*

Date	> $1 from Strike	Total Crosses	(H − L) / C	Strikes Crossed	Closing Distance to Strike ($)	Open ($)	Close ($)
2007/09/21	292	0	0.030	0	−0.85	141.14	144.15
2007/10/19	341	1	0.027	1	0.42	174.24	170.42
2007/11/16	136	35	0.046	2	1.39	165.30	166.39
2007/12/21	354	1	0.021	1	−1.09	190.12	193.91
2008/01/18	210	41	0.038	2	1.36	161.71	161.36
2008/02/15	60	20	0.024	1	−0.37	126.27	124.63
2008/03/20	92	37	0.031	1	−1.73	131.12	133.27
2008/04/18	179	3	0.024	1	1.04	159.12	161.04
2008/05/16	349	6	0.018	1	−2.38	190.11	187.62
2008/06/20	298	1	0.034	2	0.27	179.35	175.27
2008/07/18	274	2	0.028	1	0.15	168.52	165.15
2008/08/15	262	0	0.027	0	0.74	179.04	175.74
Average (abs)			0.029		0.98		
Total	2,847	147					
Ratio	19.37						

As mentioned earlier, Apple exhibits unusual expiration day behavior as revealed by the high ratio of minutes more than $1 from a strike to minutes containing a strike price cross (19.37). The elevated value of this metric reflects a very low percentage chance of the stock crossing a strike price during any particular minute of the trading day. As revealed in the table, 8 of 12 expirations had 6 or fewer crosses during the entire 390 minutes of trading. However, this number is contrasted by the average close to strike price distance, which was the smallest of the group ($0.98). Furthermore, Apple's average high-low percentage is unremarkable (2.9% of the closing price). The correct analysis combines all four data items: minutes trading more than $1 from a strike price, minutes containing a strike price cross, average high-low span, and average closing distance from a strike price. Using this information we can construct a reasonable picture of the stock's behavior. We know, for example, from the high-low ratio that the stock tends to trade within a restricted range averaging less than 3% of its closing price. During most of the day, this range does not cross a strike price (thus the small number of total crosses). Although the 2.9% high-low span averages $4.73, the stock tends to return to a more restricted range near the close. Surprisingly, minute-by-minute analysis reveals that only 16 of the 147 strike crosses listed in the table (10.9%) occurred during the final hour of trading.

The picture that emerges includes trading across a 3% range that narrows near the close as the stock approaches, but does not cross, a strike price. Dividing the average closing distance ($0.98) by the average closing price ($163.29) yields a final range of just 0.6%. Because most strike crosses occur earlier in the day when the stock is more active, long straddles are often a profitable trade. Further minute-by-minute analysis reveals that 38% of the strike crosses occur before 12:00 and 76% before 14:00. Understanding that the stock is likely to return to a more restricted range also leads to the conclusion that profitable long trades should be closed early. In most cases, holding these trades beyond 14:00 would reduce or completely eliminate all profit. This problem frequently surfaces when traders count on pinning behavior and mistakenly believe that a rising or falling stock is migrating to the next strike price. In most cases, it makes sense to close a winning long position with a modest profit, which, on expiration day, is commonly more than 50%. We will return to this discussion in the context of specific trades, and it will be evident that opening and closing the same trade several times can often result in spectacular profits as a stock migrates away from and back to a strike price.

TABLE 2.6   *MasterCard, Summary Data for 12 Expirations (Quarterly earnings were not released before any of the expirations in the table.)*

Date	> $1 from Strike	Total Crosses	(H − L) / C	Strikes Crossed	Closing Distance to Strike ($)	Open ($)	Close ($)
2007/09/21	233	5	0.037	1	1.56	150.90	146.56
2007/10/19	357	0	0.024	0	1.60	153.25	151.60
2007/11/16	234	21	0.041	2	−0.13	186.00	184.87
2007/12/21	208	61	0.041	1	2.35	209.77	212.35
2008/01/18	102	91	0.036	1	−0.38	178.58	174.62
2008/02/15	173	36	0.044	1	−4.00	200.59	206.00
2008/03/20	220	33	0.091	2	0.38	206.60	220.38
2008/04/18	385	0	0.031	0	3.71	234.40	233.71
2008/05/16	381	0	0.029	0	3.40	288.00	283.40
2008/06/20	252	10	0.040	1	4.01	290.00	284.01
2008/07/18	218	48	0.033	1	0.86	285.38	280.86
2008/08/15	337	1	0.018	1	−1.05	236.91	238.95
Average (abs)			0.039		1.95		
Total	3,100	306					
Ratio	10.13						

Although MasterCard did not display consistent pinning effects during the year profiled, some expirations displayed strong strike price effects. Three expirations—November 2007, January 2008, and March 2008—each ended with the stock trading near a strike price. Two of these expirations, November 2007 and March 2008, involved more than a single strike. In November, the stock opened at $186 and climbed slightly to $186.99 before falling below both the $185 and $180 strikes. After 14:40, the price rose quickly, crossing the $180 strike and climbing nearly $5 to close only $0.13 below $185. Figure 2.2 displays the minute-by-minute profile for this expiration.

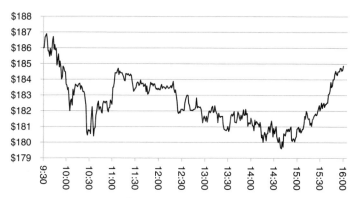

FIGURE 2.2   *Minute-by-minute trading profile for MasterCard on November 16, 2007. Although the stock experiences strike price effects and closes near the $185 strike, pinning never occurs. Time is displayed on the x-axis, price on the y-axis.*

This chart illustrates the difference between pinning and other strike price effects. Pinning would have involved trading in a narrow range above and below the

$185 strike. However, it was clear in the final few minutes that the stock was migrating toward the strike price. At-the-money long straddles purchased early in the day when the stock crossed $185 and then later in the day at $180 would have both been profitable. In the second case, at 14:57 with approximately one hour remaining, options were relatively inexpensive; the $180 call traded for $0.65, and the $180 put for $0.50. At the close, the calls traded for $4.60. The straddle, originally purchased for $1.15, gained 300%. Furthermore, the trade was a rational choice because the stock did not display pinning behavior when it briefly touched the $180 strike, and the risk was confined to a small amount of time decay in the value of the options.

The March 2008 expiration was considerably different in that the stock steadily migrated directly to a strike price, where it remained for 2.5 hours until the final close. Figure 2.3 displays the complete profile.

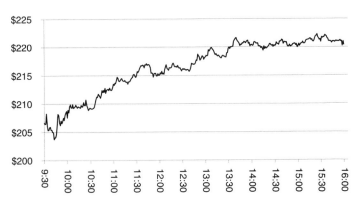

FIGURE 2.3   *Minute-by-minute trading profile for MasterCard on March 20, 2008. The stock pinned to the $220 strike at 13:30, where it remained until the close. Time is displayed on the x-axis, price on the y-axis.*

This profile supports many different types of trades, including long $210 straddles initiated early in the day, covered calls, several possible ratios using $205, $210, and $220 calls, and naked short $220 straddles placed after pinning commenced at 13:30. The decision to choose one trade over another must necessarily depend on several factors, including risk tolerance, account size, collateral requirements, and most important, preference of the trader. For example, an investor who was willing to purchase a strangle consisting of $200 puts and $210 calls at 9:41 when the stock crossed the $205 midpoint would have risked $1.80 because both options were likely to expire worthless. However, the risk of such a trade is purely related to slow time and volatility decay and the position can be closed at any time. Held until the closing bell, the call side would have been worth $10.40, and the trade would have delivered a 478% profit. A more conservative investor might have waited until the pinning effect was apparent and initiated a ratio trade. Purchasing $210 calls for $10 at 13:33 and selling three times as many $220 calls for $1.45 would have created a position that was net long $5.65. At the close, with the short $220 calls worth just $0.45, the position would have been long $8.65 (a 53% profit). Finally, a simple short $220 straddle that sold for $3.10 ($1.45 call/$1.65 put) at 13:33 was worth just $0.45 at the close (an 85% profit).

Of the three trades, the long straddle was the easiest to manage while also being the most profitable. However, you should not forget that the dominant expiration day forces—implied volatility collapse and time decay—tend to work against the trade. The ratio trade, which benefits from these forces, was also easy to manage. The long side, constructed with deep in-the-money calls, exhibited no time decay and effectively hedged the short side. At expiration, the position would have been buffered against a $4.35 move to the downside (the revenue obtained by selling $220 calls), and a $2.18 move to the upside (the break-even point where profit from the long side equals the loss on the short side).[3] For most investors, either of these approaches is favorable to a purely short position because these become increasingly sensitive to small movements of the stock as the closing bell approaches. In the final few minutes, a $0.50 underlying price change will more than double the cost to repurchase the losing side of a naked short straddle. This dynamic makes it increasingly important to tighten stops as time progresses, and to close positions that are moving in either direction.

The January expiration also exhibited significant pinning behavior that began around 14:30. However, the shape of the minute-by-minute profile was considerably more complex in January than it was in March. Beginning at noon, the stock traded above and below the strike within a range of approximately $1. The oscillations gradually narrowed until the stock clearly pinned around 14:30. From this point on, underlying price changes were limited to just a few cents. Once again, the combination of a steadily narrowing trading range and accelerating implied volatility collapse near the end of the trading day enhanced the probability of success for short straddles and ratios. Figure 2.4 displays the complete profile.

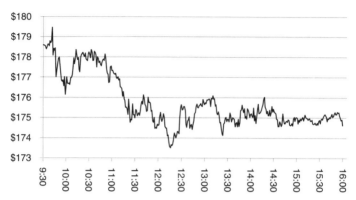

FIGURE 2.4   *Minute-by-minute trading profile for MasterCard on January 18, 2008. The stock began to oscillate around the strike price at 12:00 and finally pinned around 14:30. From this point on, the stock traded in a very narrow range. Time is displayed on the x-axis, price on the y-axis.*

On this particular trading day, because of the large number of oscillations around the $175 strike, each minute had a 23% chance of containing a strike cross. The total number of crosses (91) is the largest on any of the lists. In addition, the number of minutes more than $1 away from a strike shrank to 102—the lowest value for MasterCard in the 12-expiration time frame. Unfortunately, a long straddle placed at the time of the first strike cross would have failed because the magnitude of the stock move was too small to generate a profit. At 12:02, when the stock traded at the $175 strike, an at-the-money straddle traded for $3.05 ($160 call/$1.45 put). A few minutes later, at 12:19, with the stock at $173.70, the trade was worth only $2.84 ($0.84 call/$2.00 put). In the next few minutes, it reversed direction and returned to the $175 strike (12:28). The best decision would have been to close the position at this time with a small loss (the options traded for $1.40 call/$1.40 put).

The more reliable ratio trade, which depends on falling implied volatility and is hedged against underlying price changes, would have been a better choice. At 12:02, when the stock crossed the $175 strike, a 1:3 ratio trade consisting of long $170 calls and short $175 calls would have been net long $0.20 ($5.00 for the long $170 calls − $1.60 × 3 for the short $175 calls). The trade would have delivered steady profit as implied volatility fell and time decay eroded the option prices. At the closing bell, the long $170 calls traded for $4.60, and the short $175 calls could have been repurchased for $0.10. The position would have been net long $4.30, and the total profit would have been $4.10 from an investment of only $0.20. The ratio trade was an excellent choice because it had virtually no downside risk (the short side paid for the entire cost of the long side), and was somewhat hedged by the long $170 calls against an upside move of the stock. In this regard, the trade would have returned a profit even if the stock climbed $1.60 because the long side would have gained $1.60 and the short side would have been worth its original sale price.

For comparison, an investor who decided to sell naked puts and calls when the stock returned to the $175 strike at 12:28 would have generated profit of $2.30. (The straddle sold for $2.80 at 12:28, and only $0.50 at 16:00.) This trade also delivered steady profit and was hedged against a $2.80 move in either direction. Despite its success, the trade was a poor choice. Pure naked short positions are safer late in the day when implied volatility collapses quickly. Waiting until 14:00 when the stock began to stabilize would have generated $1.75 of option premium ($1.00 call/$0.75 put). Accelerated implied volatility collapse is evident in the minute-by-minute option price history, which reveals a straddle price of only $1.45 at 14:18 (18 minutes later) when the stock spiked $1 to the upside. Earlier in the day, the same spike would have resulted in a paper loss; a conservative investor might have been forced to stop out. Held until the closing bell, the smaller late trade would have generated a respectable $1.25 profit. (The straddle traded for $0.50 at the close.) As previously mentioned, it makes statistical sense to initiate trades that rely on option price decay late in the day and trades that profit from large price changes during the midday implied volatility stability window. Ratios fall in the middle because they have both long and short components. These trades are especially effective when a stock trades above or below a strike and there is opportunity to collect option premium on the short side while generating profit on the long side. Many other strategies are also possible, including initiating a smaller ratio and adding short contracts when the stock spikes beyond the strike price. It is also possible to leverage oscillations around a strike price to profitably leg out of a trade. The short side of a call ratio can be closed on a downtick and the long side on an uptick.

By following a few simple but statistically sound rules, we can construct highly profitable positions for heavily traded stocks like MasterCard even when they fail to display strike price effects. In most cases, an effective strategy is to purchase long straddles relatively early in the day if the stock crosses a strike price. Figure 2.5 displays minute-by-minute closing prices for MasterCard on such a day.

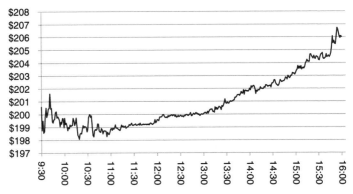

FIGURE 2.5   *Minute-by-minute trading profile for MasterCard on February 15, 2008. The stock briefly exhibited strike price effects when it traded very close to $200 for about 1 hour before decoupling and climbing another $6. A long $200 straddle placed during this time frame was highly profitable. Time is displayed on the x-axis, and price on the y-axis.*

At 13:00, with MasterCard trading at $200, at-the-money straddles were $1.93 ($0.98 call/$0.95 put). At the closing bell, with the stock trading at $206, the call side of the straddle sold for $6.20 (a 221% profit). The lack of any significant reversal between initiation of the trade and the closing bell would have caused most investors to hold the trade until the very end and realize the maximum profit.

Like the other stocks, Research in Motion displays varying degrees of strike price effects from one expiration to the next. However, even expirations where no pinning is evident are characterized by some attraction to a large open interest strike. October 2007 is an excellent example. As revealed in Table 2.7, the stock opened more than $2 above a strike, but immediately fell back to cross the $115 boundary early in the day. Although the stock never pinned to the strike, it crossed four different times, ultimately closing within $0.03.

TABLE 2.7   Research in Motion, Summary Data for 12 Expirations (The company released earnings on 12/20/2007 after the market close. Expiration Friday was the next day. This event is shaded gray.)

Date	> $1 from Strike	Total Crosses	(H − L) / C	Strikes Crossed	Closing Distance to Strike ($)	Open ($)	Close ($)
2007/09/21	390	0	0.022	0	-1.82	91.43	93.18
2007/10/19	45	34	0.033	1	-0.03	117.33	114.97
2007/11/16	217	35	0.106	2	-2.43	104.15	107.57
2007/12/21	150	9	0.049	1	-1.37	122.16	118.63
2008/01/18	175	18	0.052	1	-1.42	88.97	88.58
2008/02/15	56	34	0.020	1	0.19	94.22	95.19
2008/03/20	174	40	0.061	2	-0.06	101.48	104.94
2008/04/18	251	0	0.036	0	-1.78	121.75	123.22
2008/05/16	157	1	0.020	1	0.36	141.67	140.36
2008/06/20	20	22	0.025	1	-0.44	145.76	144.56
2008/07/18	159	9	0.073	2	-2.15	109.55	112.85
2008/08/15	158	21	0.039	1	-1.20	131.70	128.80
Average (abs)			0.045		1.10		
Total	1952	223					
Ratio	8.75						

Figure 2.6 displays minute-by-minute closing prices for the October 2007 expiration.

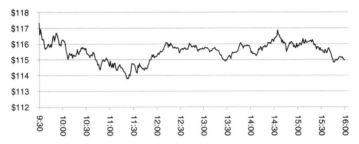

FIGURE 2.6   *Minute-by-minute closing prices for Research in Motion on expiration Friday, October 19, 2007. Although the stock never exhibited classic pinning behavior, it crossed the strike 4 times and closed within $0.03. Time is displayed on the x-axis, and price on the y-axis.*

The large body of academic research on pinning counts this expiration in the positive column. However, that characterization is misleading, as evidenced by the dramatic differences between this figure and Figures 2.3 and 2.4. In Figure 2.3, we saw the stock rise to the strike price, where it remained for 2.5 hours until the close. In Figure 2.4, the stock fell to a strike price and continued oscillating above and below until the range of the oscillation decreased to just a few cents. This particular expiration was characterized by the largest number of strike price crosses (91) in the group.

Despite the lack of true pinning, strike price effects and implied volatility collapse dominated to create several different trading opportunities. The simplest would have been a simple ratio trade initiated when the stock first crossed the $115 strike at 10:55. A trade that was long $110 calls and short three times as many $115 calls would have had an initial long value of $2.35 ($5.05 long call / 3 × $0.90 short call). At the closing bell, we could have repurchased the short calls for $0.05 ($0.15 total), and sold the long side for its initial price of $5.05. The trade would, therefore, have generated a $2.55 profit. Conversely, only one of the strike crosses yielded a profitable straddle (the 13:30 cross). A long straddle purchased at the 10:55 cross would have cost $1.80. This value was exactly maintained through the 11:22 modest price drop to $113.78. Conversely, purchasing a straddle at the 13:30 cross for $1.20 would have yielded a modest profit of $0.80 at 14:35, when the stock reached its last peak of $116.87. A determined investor who stopped out of the first long straddle would have generated a 67% profit with the second.

The December 2007 earnings-driven expiration exhibited dramatically different dynamics. There was no evidence of pinning, and strike price effects were very limited. One marked difference between the October and December 2007 expirations was the ratio between the number of minutes trading further than $1 from a strike price and the number of minutes containing a strike cross. In October, the ratio was only 1.3; in

December the value climbed to 16.7. The low percentage of minutes containing a strike price cross is strong evidence for the lack of strike price effects. Despite these dynamics, a 1:3 ratio trade initiated when the stock crossed $120 at 9:39 generated substantial profit at the close. For example, we could have purchased $115 calls for $5.50 and sold three times as many $120 calls for $1.75. The total trade would have been initially long $0.25 ($5.50 − 3 × $1.75). When the closing bell rang, the short side was worth just $0.05, and the long side traded for $3.55. The position could, therefore, have been closed for $3.40 ($3.55 − 3 × $0.05). The tremendous profit of this trade testifies to the protective nature of the short calls, which buffered the long side of the trade against a decline from $5.50 to $3.55.

Following statistical inference and investing in a long straddle at the 9:39 strike cross would have also been profitable. The initial cost would have been $3.34 ($1.75 call/$1.59 put), and the trade could have been closed at 10:10, when the stock fell to $116.53 for $4.28 ($0.53 call/$3.75 put). The trade would have generated 28% profit in only 30 minutes. These dynamics fit well with the low at-the-money ratio mentioned previously. Many stocks display this characteristic on expiration days that immediately follow an earnings announcement, especially if the stock reacted by moving through more than one strike price in the after- or before-hours session.

The Evening before Expiration

Extending this discussion, we can construct summary tables describing the magnitude of overnight price changes for each stock. This information can be used to structure trades the evening before expiration. The dynamics are complex because, as mentioned in Chapter 1, the market accommodates large overnight time decay with lower implied volatility and widened bid-ask spreads. In general terms, however, these adjustments are insufficient to overcome the large amount of option premium that is lost in the final evening before expiration. Ratios and other short positions can often be structured to capitalize on this distortion, especially for stocks that tend to migrate to a nearby strike price. However, because price distortions are usually subtle, it is important to have some view of the potential overnight change before initiating a trade.

Table 2.8 summarizes overnight behavior on the evening preceding expiration for the five stocks that we have been following. The data excludes records that immediately follow quarterly earnings announcements. This information is displayed separately in Table 2.9. Although Goldman Sachs had three earnings announcements that preceded expiration, only the September 2007 event is excluded, because the others had a gap of at least one trading day.

TABLE 2.8   *Final Evening Price Change Summaries for Five Heavily Traded Stocks (Quarterly announcements that immediately preceded expiration have been excluded.)*

Stock	Avg. (Day-1) Close Dist. to Strike ($)	Avg. Exp. Day Open Dist. to Strike ($)	Avg. C->O $ (Abs. Val.)	Avg. C-> O % (Abs. Val.)
AAPL	1.05	1.56	1.59	1.0%
GOOG	1.58	4.26	4.15	0.7%
GS	1.82	2.53	1.75	0.9%
MA	2.04	2.13	1.78	0.8%
RIMM	1.28	1.88	1.30	1.2%

Avg. C->O is average close to open.

TABLE 2.9   *Final Evening Price Change Behavior for Three of the Five Stocks Listed in Table 2.8 on Days That Immediately Followed Quarterly Earnings Announcements (The other two stocks listed in Table 2.8, AAPL and MA, do not appear in this table because they did not have any quarterly earnings announcements coincident with options expiration.)*

Stock	Exp. Day	Day-1 Close	Exp. Day Open	Abs Value (C->O)	(C->O) Percent
GOOG	2007/10/19	639.62	654.56	14.94	2.3%
GOOG	2008/04/18	449.54	535.21	85.67	19.1%
GOOG	2008/07/18	533.44	498.35	35.09	6.6%
GS	2007/09/21	203.53	205.56	2.03	1.0%
RIMM	2007/12/21	106.99	122.16	15.17	14.2%

Close-to-open values listed in columns 4 and 5 of Table 2.8 suggest that average overnight price changes are relatively modest in the absence of quarterly earnings.

As might be expected, the changes are almost always larger after an earnings announcement (Table 2.9). Google, for example, exhibited $15, $85, and $35 price swings from close to open after its three earnings releases, and Research in Motion experienced a $15 price change after its single announcement. The March 2007 overnight price change listed for Goldman Sachs was much more modest.

The information suggests that, absent an earnings announcement, carefully structured short positions designed to profit from overnight time decay on the final evening should be profitable for these stocks. Forward ratios that are long the near strike and short the far strike are often a good choice because the far strike is disproportionately affected by time decay when expiration is very close. Selecting situations where the short side pays for all or most of the long side increases the potential profit and decreases the risk associated with a large underlying price change in either direction. Table 2.10 illustrates this concept with structured trades for the first four Apple Computer expirations listed in the previous tables, September 2007 through December 2007.

TABLE 2.10 *Ratio Trades for Four Consecutive Apple Computer Expirations (Option and stock prices were selected at the close on Thursday and the open on expiration Friday. All four trades were structured as 1:2 ratios.)*

Date	Stock ($)	Strikes (Long/Short)	Long Call ($)	Short Call ($)	Ratio	Net ($)	Profit/Loss ($)
2007/09/20	140.31	135/140	5.34	0.95	1:2	3.44	
2007/09/21	141.14	135/140	6.30	1.45	1:2	3.40	−0.04
2007/10/18	173.50	170/175	3.85	0.86	1:2	2.13	
2007/10/19	174.24	170/175	4.35	0.88	1:2	2.59	0.46
2007/11/15	164.30	165/170	1.84	0.88	1:2	0.08	
2007/11/16	165.30	165/170	1.96	0.31	1:2	1.34	1.26
2007/12/20	187.21	185/190	2.90	0.37	1:2	2.16	
2007/12/21	190.12	185/190	5.30	1.02	1:2	3.26	1.10

The first entry in each pair displays parameters for the trade at the market close on Thursday, including the final option trade. The second entry represents trade values at the open the next morning, expiration Friday. Opening option prices were recorded at the time of the very first option trade.

Pricing of the very first trade can occasionally be misleading because of distortions that result from large overnight price swings. In some instances, an investor suffering a large loss will overpay to quickly close a trade; in others, an investor with a large profit might accept a reduced price to quickly capture the gain. Most often, the culprit is a "market" order placed before the opening bell. In addition, timing and synchronization is always a complex issue because options are less liquid than stocks. The analyses presented in these pages attempt to reduce the impact of these discrepancies by selecting heavily traded stocks with large options open interest. Furthermore, each of the situations discussed in this particular section involved heavy trading during the premarket session because the results followed quarterly earnings. Heavy premarket trading volumes contribute to liquidity and fair pricing at the open. For this discussion, therefore, the most reasonable approach is to measure overnight price changes against the first opening option trade.

The trades outlined in Table 2.10 are structured as 1:2 call ratios where the short side contains twice as many contracts as the long side, and the short strike is farther out-of-the-money. The Net column displays actual trade values at the close on Thursday and the open on Friday.

Scanning down the Profit/Loss column, it is clear that the November trade generated more profit than the others. The reason relates to strike price selection. Each of the other three structures includes long in-the-money and a short out-of-the-money option; that is, the trade straddles the closing price of the stock. With the short strike relatively close and the long strike already in the money, the trade is poorly hedged against a large upward price spike. Some of the problem is related to the deltas of the two options. The delta of the long in-the-money calls will increase more slowly than the delta of the short out-of-the-money calls in response to an upward movement of the stock. Furthermore, because the initial structures are net long, they are not protected against large downward price spikes. If the stock falls sharply and all the options lose their value, each of the net long trades will become worthless, and the initial investment will be lost.

The November trade avoids these problems with strike prices that are both out-of-the-money. Because both sides of the trade are approximately equal in cost, a large downward spike that collapses both option values will not result in a loss. (The initial net trade cost is only $0.08.) Conversely, the stock can climb $5 and still generate a large profit on the long side while the short side expires worthless. For a modest price increase, the opening option prices on Friday will tend to exaggerate these differences with the short side losing value and the long side gaining. Once again, option deltas are the key. As the long side crosses the strike price, its delta rises quickly. In the case of the November calls, the long side gained $0.12, and the short side lost $0.57. Because the short side was twice as large, the total difference was $1.26.

This effect is more dramatic in Table 2.11, which displays results for the same trades using 1:3 ratios.

TABLE 2.11   *Ratio Trades for Four Consecutive Apple Computer Expirations (see Table 2.10) (Option and stock prices were selected at the close on Thursday and the open on expiration Friday. All four trades were structured as 1:3 ratios.)*

Date	Stock ($)	Strikes (Long/Short)	Long Call ($)	Short Call ($)	Ratio	Net ($)	Profit/Loss ($)
2007/09/20	140.31	135/140	5.34	0.95	1:3	2.49	
2007/09/21	141.14	135/140	6.30	1.45	1:3	1.95	−0.54
2007/10/18	173.50	170/175	3.85	0.86	1:3	1.27	
2007/10/19	174.24	170/175	4.35	0.88	1:3	1.71	0.44
2007/11/15	164.30	165/170	1.84	0.88	1:3	−0.80	
2007/11/16	165.30	165/170	1.96	0.31	1:3	1.03	1.83
2007/12/20	187.21	185/190	2.90	0.37	1:3	1.79	
2007/12/21	190.12	185/190	5.30	1.02	1:3	2.24	0.45

Using larger ratios exaggerates the effects of weak trade structures and benefits the strong ones. Most notably, the December trade lost almost all of its profit, whereas the November trade gained value. Had the stock price fallen sharply, the more favorable November trade would have still returned an $0.80 profit. In the reverse case, an underlying price increase of another $5 to $170 would have resulted in $3.97 of additional profit at the close on Friday. The total return would have been $5.80 because the long side would have risen to a value of $5, the short side would have expired worthless, and the $0.80 premium of the original position would have been realized as profit. The absolute break-even point for this trade, including the $0.80 premium of the initial position, is $172.90.[4] The trade, therefore, was structured to generate profit across a very large range from the lowest possible underlying stock price, to a price more than $7 higher than Friday's open.

Many investors would be tempted to continue this trade until the final close. In this particular case, that strategy would have been successful because the stock climbed to $166.39, yielding a net position value of $1.39 (an additional $0.36). The difference was very small because the long calls opened $0.30 in-the-money with $1.66 of excess time premium ($1.96 - $0.30). That $1.66 was lost throughout the day. The underlying price increase of $1.09 coupled with additional premium decay of $0.93 on the short side made up the difference. Generally speaking, it is wise to close profitable overnight trades at the open and begin again with new trades that are specifically structured for the final day.

In summary, for each structure the ratio selected should be based on the relationship between the price of the stock and the distance to both long and short strikes. The November trade can safely be constructed using a 1:3 ratio because both strikes are out-of-the-money and only an exceptionally large overnight move could cause a loss. The other trades should be structured using smaller ratios (1:1 or 1:2).

Finally, the data of Table 2.9 suggests that a different trading approach, designed to generate profit from large price changes, is required when expiration follows an earnings report. Long straddles are the most obvious candidate because large underlying price changes are likely and options have very little time premium remaining at the end of the expiration cycle. Surprisingly, this approach rarely works as expected. The market is efficient, and option prices generally reflect the risk of a large underlying price change. The next day when the market opens, option prices deflate quickly to reflect the new underlying stock price with implied volatility and time premium appropriate for the final trading day. Table 2.12 extends the information presented in Table 2.9 with actual option prices. As before, the first line of each pair displays closing prices on the penultimate trading day (expiration Thursday); the second line reveals opening prices on expiration Friday. The Net column displays the total trade cost, and the Profit/Loss column reflects the results that would have been obtained by closing the trade at the open on Friday.

TABLE 2.12   Long Straddles for Expirations That Immediately Follow Earnings (extension to Table 2.9)
(Information for RIMM is entered twice because two different structures are illustrated. The first line in each pair displays closing prices on expiration Thursday; the second line reveals opening prices on Friday. Out-of-the-money options were used on both sides of the Goldman Sachs example to avoid purchasing an asymmetric, very bullish $200 straddle. The trade is included here for completeness.)

Symbol	Date	Stock ($)	Strikes (Call/Put)	Call ($)	Put ($)	Total ($)	Profit/Loss ($)
GOOG	2007/10/18	639.62	640/640	14.60	17.50	32.10	
GOOG	2007/10/19	654.56	640/640	13.90	0.40	14.30	−17.80
GOOG	2008/04/17	449.54	450/450	15.30	14.70	30.00	
GOOG	2008/04/18	535.21	450/450	84.00	0.05	84.05	54.05
GOOG	2008/07/17	533.44	540/530	16.80	17.80	34.60	
GOOG	2008/07/18	498.35	540/530	0.05	29.60	29.65	−4.95
GS	2007/09/20	203.53	210/200	0.20	0.60	0.80	
GS	2007/09/21	205.56	210/200	0.30	0.15	0.45	−0.35
RIMM	2007/12/20	106.99	110/105	3.45	4.30	7.75	
RIMM	2007/12/21	122.16	110/105	11.85	0.01	11.86	4.11
RIMM	2007/12/20	106.99	105/105	6.20	4.30	10.50	
RIMM	2007/12/21	122.16	105/105	14.90	0.01	14.91	4.41

Reading down the Profit/Loss column reveals that this strategy is flawed and very unpredictable. Two of three Google straddles lost money; the October 2007 trade lost an enormous amount despite an underlying $15 price spike. Only the April 2008 trade would have been successful, but this success resulted from a 19% price spike of more than $85 (approximately 8 standard deviations measured against implied volatility at that time). An alternative strategy, favored by some investors, involves purchasing very inexpensive far out-of-the-money strangles with the hope that the stock will exhibit a price spike not comprehended in the prices of contracts at distant strikes. The expectation is that most trades will lose all their value, but that an occasional outsized spike will return enough money to more than compensate for losses. Following this strategy for the already profitable April 2008 expiration might have involved purchasing $530 calls and $370 puts for $0.60 ($0.10 call/$0.50 put). After the announcement, the position traded for $7.75 ($7.70 call/$0.05 put). The percentage gain was much larger than that of the at-the-money $450 straddle (1,183% versus 180%).

The strategy is worth exploring in more detail. More specifically, it would be helpful to know whether any of the losing trades could have been made profitable by replacing at-the-money options with more distant strikes. For example, had we purchased out-of-the-money $650 calls and $630 puts for the October 2007 Google expiration we would have paid $24.20 ($11.60 call/$12.60 put). The trade would have still lost because the $15 underlying price change resulted in a final position value of only $7.10 ($6.60 call/$0.50 put). Further out-of-the-money options experienced even large price collapses because the stock settled between the strikes. (A $660/$620 strangle collapsed from $16.60 to $1.70.) In summary, the price of a $10 out-of-the-money strangle comprehended a $34 underlying price change, and the price of a $20 out-of-the-money strangle was designed to absorb a $37 price spike. None of the choices were profitable.

The same dynamics held true for the final Google expiration on the list (July 2008). Significantly widening the strangle by purchasing $570 calls and $500 puts resulted in a larger loss. The position value fell from $13.00 ($6.50 call/$6.50 put) to $7.55 ($0.05 call/$7.50 put) with the stock opening approximately $2 in-the-money on the put side. The value of these options was designed to comprehend a $46 underlying price decline to $487. As might be expected, wider spacings composed of options that remained out-of-the-money after the overnight price change exhibited worse performance. The $590 call/$480 put trade collapsed from $5.40 to $1.20. (Initial prices were $2.60 call/$2.80 put, final prices were $0.05 call/$1.15 put.) Price distortions grow larger at the extremes—these options were priced to absorb a $58 underlying price change.

Wider spacing was not a solution for the Goldman Sachs example because the price change was very small and the existing position was already too wide. Alternatively, an at-the-money $200 straddle would have been profitable with the position value rising from $4.60 to $5.55. However, this trade was avoided because it was extremely asymmetric ($4.00 call/$0.60 put). It would have been a directional bet that can be thought of as purchasing in-the-money calls and hedging with inexpensive out-of-the-money puts. Only a very bullish investor would have initiated this trade, which would have lost large amounts of money had the stock price fallen. Many other trade structures would have accomplished the same goals.

Finally, both at-the-money and out-of-the-money trades would have succeeded for Research in Motion. Table 2.12 illustrates with an example of each. Further widening the trade with $115 calls and $100 puts increased the profit in both percentage and absolute terms. The new values were $4.28 for the initial position ($1.75 call/$2.53 put) and $6.90 at the open on Friday morning ($6.85 call/$0.05 put), a 61% profit. A very wide trade composed of $120 calls and $90 puts returned an even larger profit of 90%. The initial position would have cost $1.33 ($0.67 call/$0.66 put); after the overnight price change, the calls traded for $2.49, and the puts traded for $0.04.

In summary, there is no consistent strategy for generating profit from the price distortions of an earnings-associated expiration. In situations where the options market mistakenly underprices risk, tremendous opportunities exist on the long side. For long straddles, the profit, measured in percentage terms, increases sharply when distant strike prices are selected. For the April 2008 Google example, the widest possible spacing yielded a profit of 1,183% versus 180% for an at-the-money straddle. Risk also increases for these trades because both sides can open out-of-the-money on expiration day with just a few hours remaining. Note, however, that at-the-money straddles also lose tremendous value in the inevitable implied volatility collapse. For example, in the October 2007 Google expiration, an at-the-money $640 straddle lost $17.80, while a far out-of-the-money $660/$620 strangle lost $14.90. Measured in percentage terms, the loss was 55% for the straddle and 90% for the wide strangle. When a fixed amount of money is being invested, thinner spacing is safer, and wider spacing provides more leverage.

When the market overprices risk, simple long structures such as straddles lose money. Purchasing more distant strike prices exaggerates the problem. The examples outlined previously reveal that options can be dramatically overpriced. Relatively expensive options at distant strike prices can collapse to worthless when the market reopens after earnings are announced. Many investors have attempted to capitalize on the more common overpriced scenario by selling calls and puts at distant strikes. This strategy inevitably self-destructs when the inevitable 8 standard deviation price spike occurs. The December 2007 RIMM and April 2008 GOOG expirations serve as excellent examples. In all, two of five earnings-associated expirations ended with outsized price spikes that were not comprehended by the options market. The next chapter explores additional trade structures that are better suited to these situations.

Summary

The dominant forces that characterize options expiration—accelerated time decay, implied volatility collapse, and migration to a strike price—manifest themselves in slightly different ways for different stocks and expirations. The well-known dynamic of pinning is an oversimplification; a more precise picture emerges from statistics about the frequency and number of strike price crossings and the number of minutes that a stock trades more than a certain distance from a strike. In some instances, a stock will cross multiple strike price boundaries before settling very close to a single strike. In others, a stock will remain close to a single strike for most of the day before decoupling and moving away. Both situations can be very confusing if closing distance to a strike price is the only metric used. Moreover, an investor who relies on limited information is likely to choose the wrong trade. In this regard the behavior of a stock around expiration is best understood at the minute-by-minute level of granularity.

Expirations that closely follow an earnings announcement are special because the options market responds to these events by pricing large amounts of risk into option contracts. For a given stock in a particular expiration, relative distance to strike prices and implied volatility are important parameters that determine whether a reasonable trade exists. More often than not, risk is overpriced. However, selling naked calls and puts (even far out-of-the-money) to capitalize on this distortion is risky because many earnings are characterized by outsized price spikes not comprehended in option prices.

In the next chapter, we explore a variety of expiration-specific trading strategies. The discussion focuses on different time frames, including the second-to-last day and three different segments of the final day.

Endnotes

1. In this analysis, a stock is considered to have traded more than $1 from a strike price only if both the high and low of the minute were more than $1 from the strike.

2. During the 12 months represented in Table 2.2, MasterCard traded 4,665 minutes on expiration days, and Apple traded 4,680 minutes.

3. The break-even point is calculated as follows: $X = 3(X - \$1.45)$, where X is the increase in the underlying stock price. The left side of the equation (X) is the profit for the long side, and the right side $3(X - \$1.45)$ is the loss on the short side when the calls are repurchased.

4. The formula for calculating the break-even point for this trade is created by setting the short side equal to the long side. If X is the final closing price of the stock, the short side value is given by $3(X - 170) + 0.80$, and the long side is equal to $X - 165$. Therefore $3(X - 170) + 0.80 = X - 165$. Solving for X yields a price of $172.90.

Chapter 3

Day Trading Strategies

Expiration Thursday

In Chapter 1, "Expiration Pricing Dynamics," we saw that the amount of overnight time decay experienced by an option contract rises sharply as the final trading day approaches. Time decay is a simple dynamic. Because the options market is open for 6.5 hours each day and closed for 17.5 hours, the percentage of value lost each evening while the market is closed rapidly increases until, on the evening before the final trading day, 31.3% of the remaining time is lost. As mentioned earlier, the market anticipates these price distortions and responds with a combination of implied volatility swings and widely varying bid-ask spreads. Buyers respond to escalating overnight time decay by lowering their bids, while sellers fight to keep prices high enough to compensate for overnight event exposure. Bid-ask spreads tend to narrow and volatility tends to rise after the open each day as the underlying security becomes active. As the close approaches, volatility and bid prices both tend to fall while ask prices tend to stabilize.

We can take advantage of these dynamics to structure day trades that are opened in the morning and closed before the final bell. Day trades have a distinct advantage because they can be closed at any time. Option trades designed to profit from time decay cannot normally be executed in a single day because the amount of decay between 9:30 and 16:00 is insignificant. Thursday and Friday of expiration week are exceptions. However, time decay is only a small part of the story. Most of the option value decay that occurs during these two sessions is related to implied volatility collapse rather than time decay. Table 3.1 displays time dynamics for the final two trading days of an expiration cycle. The fourth column—percentage of a year remaining—plugs directly into Black-Scholes and other pricing formulas.

TABLE 3.1   *Time Dynamics for the Final Two Days of an Options Cycle (Equity and index options expire Saturday evening at 23:59.)*

Day	Time	Days Remaining	% Year Remaining
Thursday	9:30	2.60	0.71%
Thursday	16:00	2.33	0.64%
Friday	9:30	1.60	0.44%
Friday	16:00	1.33	0.37%

If time decay were the dominant force, we would expect an at-the-money option contract to lose only a small amount of its value on either of the two final days. In actual trading, option prices collapse to their in-the-money value on expiration Friday. Thursday is different; option values tend to shrink enough to offset some of the time decay that must inevitably occur between the close on Thursday and the open on Friday. The actual amount is dictated by market forces that vary between stocks and expirations.

Table 3.2 displays data for a small number of representative trades designed to illustrate the pricing dynamics of expiration Thursday. Each of the trades is constructed using Apple Computer options on the Thursday immediately preceding expiration. In each case, the goal was to sell a straddle or strangle immediately after the market open, and to buy the options back at the closing bell. Therefore, option prices displayed were recorded at the opening bell and at the close of trading. The table is organized into sets of four entries. Each set contains opening call and put prices (first pair of entries), followed by closing call and put prices (second pair of entries). Columns 8 and 9 provide underlying pricing data, implied volatility and delta.

In situations where the underlying stock moves only a small amount, at-the-money straddles provide the largest opportunity. The September 2007 expiration featured in the first group serves as an excellent example because the stock drifted away from the strike price, fell to $139.32, climbed to $141.79, and ultimately returned to close at $140.31. Both sides lost significant value. Sometimes, however, movement of the stock can preferentially increase the gain on one side. November 2007 (group 3) was chosen as an example of this phenomenon. Both trades provided excellent returns (46% and 33%, respectively).

TABLE 3.2 Trades Designed to Exploit Pricing Dynamics on Expiration Thursday (Each of the four examples is constructed using Apple Computer options on expiration Thursday. The first trade is an at-the-money straddle, the remaining are strangles [different strikes]. Strangles were selected whenever the stock opened between two strike prices. The put side of the November 2007 trade is highlighted to emphasize its declining price, which seems counterintuitive in light of a falling stock price, as discussed in the text. Implied volatilities and deltas were calculated using a 1.5% risk-free interest rate.)

Date/Time	Stock	Strike	Opt.	Price	Total	Gain	Implied Volatility	Delta
2007/09/20 9:30	140.15	140	C	1.55			0.31	0.52
2007/09/20 9:30	140.15	140	P	1.40	2.95		0.31	-0.48
2007/09/20 16:00	140.31	140	C	0.95			0.17	0.57
2007/09/20 16:00	140.31	140	P	0.65	1.60	1.35	0.18	-0.43
2007/10/18 9:30	171.50	175	C	0.69			0.34	0.23
2007/10/18 9:30	171.50	170	P	1.23	1.92		0.33	-0.38
2007/10/18 16:00	173.50	175	C	0.86			0.27	0.35
2007/10/18 16:00	173.50	170	P	0.42	1.28	0.64	0.29	-0.19
2007/11/15 9:30	166.39	170	C	1.46			0.51	0.33
2007/11/15 9:30	166.39	165	P	2.76	4.22		0.61	-0.42
2007/11/15 16:00	164.30	170	C	0.39			0.40	0.21
2007/11/15 16:00	164.30	165	P	2.42	2.81	1.41	0.39	-0.55
2008/08/14 9:30	178.33	180	C	1.23			0.32	0.37
2008/08/14 9:30	178.33	175	P	0.71	1.94		0.33	-0.24
2008/08/14 16:00	179.32	180	C	1.10			0.25	0.43
2008/08/14 16:00	179.32	175	P	0.21	1.31	0.63	0.26	-0.12

Using a Black-Scholes calculator, we can determine implied volatilities and other pricing parameters for the various components listed in the table. The analysis can clarify subtle differences. For example, understanding the price dynamics of the November 2007 trade— specifically the surprising behavior of the put side which lost value despite a $2 decline in the underlying stock price—requires a close examination of both implied volatilities and deltas. These values are listed in the final two columns of the table.

Overall, declining implied volatility dominated the intraday landscape. Each trade, regardless of strike positioning, benefited from the collapse. The first grouping provides an excellent reference point because the stock closed very near its opening price and the trade was structured with delta-sensitive at-the-money options. Implied volatility for both sides fell by nearly half from 31% to 17% (call) and 31% to 18% (put). Out-of-the-money trades also experienced noticeable implied volatility declines throughout the day. Results were consistent for both symmetric and asymmetric positions. For example, the August 2008 Apple trade (group 4) began with the stock at $178.33 and deltas of 0.37 for the $180 call and –0.24 for the $175 put. Despite this asymmetry and the selection of different strike prices, implied volatility calculations yielded nearly identical values for both sides of the initial position followed by a consistent 7% decline on both sides. The August case is a stringent test because both sides of the trade declined in value despite a $1 move of the stock in the direction of the higher delta.

Results of the November 2007 trade also become clearer in the light of calculated implied volatility and delta. At initiation, the trade was slightly asymmetric, having a call delta of 0.33 and a put delta of −0.42. This asymmetry slightly enhanced the effect of the underlying price move, causing the put to lose only $0.34, while the call lost $1.07. However, as seen in the other trades, collapsing implied volatility caused both sides to lose value; the falling stock price was insufficient to preserve the price of the puts despite their high delta and the $2 downward move. Both the November and August trades experienced underlying stock moves in the direction of the higher delta. However, the asymmetry of the November trade was smaller, and the implied volatility collapse was larger. As a result, the November trade generated a larger return.

The October 2007 trade (group 2) was also asymmetric with regard to delta. Unlike the November and August trades, however, the stock moved in the direction of the lower delta (call side). The move was large enough to reverse the deltas and generate a very small gain on the call side ($0.17); the puts lost $0.81.

Results were surprisingly consistent across both trade types and various strike price configurations. Both at- and out-of-the-money positions experienced significant value erosion. Some minor anomalies are visible in the data. For example, implied volatility of the November 2007 calls was initially 10% lower than that of the corresponding puts. Although some of these differences might be related to momentary price misalignments between stock and option markets, the trend is clear, and the results are consistent across large datasets containing many optionable stocks and spanning numerous expirations.

Unfortunately, opening and closing prices do not tell the full story. In many instances, the underlying stock exhibits transient price swings that are large enough to force conservative investors out of their trades. Figures 3.1 and 3.2 contrast the two situations. Figure 3.1 verifies the performance of the September 2007 trade by tracing intraday prices for the $140 straddle. Figure 3.2 provides contrast with intraday prices for the November 2007 strangle, which experienced very large underlying stock price changes late in the day. Both trades were ultimately profitable although they traced dramatically different paths. For comparison, each chart also traces the stock price (light gray line). Stock and option prices were recorded at the close each minute. Position values are displayed as negative numbers to reflect a short position—profit increases as the line rises.

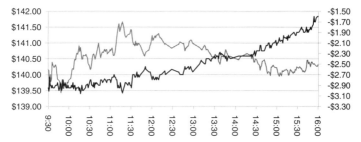

FIGURE 3.1   *Minute-by-minute value of the AAPL $140 short straddle (2007/09/20) outlined in Table 3.2. Trading price of the straddle is displayed on the right y-axis, stock price on the left y-axis, and time on the x-axis. The dark line traces the price of the option position; the light gray line traces the stock price.*

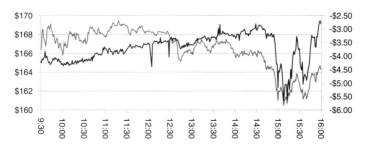

FIGURE 3.2   *Minute-by-minute value of the AAPL $165/$170 short strangle (2007/11/15) outlined in Table 3.2. Trading price of the straddle is displayed on the right y-axis, stock price on the left y-axis, and time on the x-axis. The dark line traces the price of the option position; the light gray line traces the stock price.*

As revealed in Figure 3.1, the September 2007 straddle generated a steady profit and was relatively immune to modest underlying stock price changes. It was noticeably unaffected by the $2 price swing that occurred between 10:00 and 11:30. The second trade, displayed in Figure 3.2, behaved as well as the first until a rapid downward spike that began at 14:45. Just ahead of the spike, the trade had an accumulated profit of $1.40, which grew steadily throughout the day despite a significant rise of more than $3 in the underlying stock that occurred between 10:00 and 11:00. However, at 14:58 as the price fell sharply, it crossed the break-even point. The maximum loss was sustained at 15:08, when the price climbed to $5.65. At 15:35, the stock reversed direction and began rising as quickly as it had fallen; all profit was ultimately recovered at the close.

This behavior underscores the importance of aggressively stopping out of profitable positions that begin to lose money. Unusual behavior in the options market often precedes a large underlying price spike. Such behavior is most commonly a response to breaking news. In this regard, heavily traded stocks hovering near a strike price with large options open interest are often very efficient leading indicators. Although it is difficult to draw precise conclusions, and direction is virtually impossible to predict, sharply increasing volume in the options market often precedes a large price spike. The September 2007 trade depicted in Table 3.2 turns out to be a perfect example. Just ahead of the sharpest part of the decline combined at-the-money options volume soared 500%. Figure 3.3 depicts the volume spike by charting minute-by-minute combined put and call volumes for at-the-money $165 strike price options. As before, the light gray line traces the stock price.

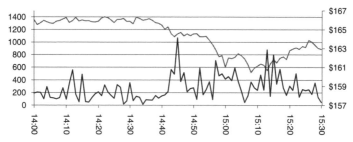

FIGURE 3.3   *Combined $165 put and call volumes versus stock price during the large downward spike visible in Figure 3.2. Combined option volume per minute is displayed on the left y-axis, stock price on the right y-axis, and time on the x-axis. The dark line traces combined volume for the $165 put and $165 call; the light gray line traces the stock price.*

The large spike visible in the chart was an excellent leading indicator because the stock continued to hover just below the $165 strike for 10 additional minutes before plunging sharply. Furthermore, the ramping option volume was noticeable in the minutes preceding the spike. Information regarding these volumes is listed in Table 3.3.

TABLE 3.3   *Option Volumes Preceding the Large Downward Spike of Figures 3.2 and 3.3*

Time	Contracts	Stock Price
14:39	111	165.65
14:40	144	165.45
14:41	160	165.02
14:42	216	165.26
14:43	562	164.55
14:44	490	164.23
14:45	1065	164.54

Looking at the data it becomes clear that the large volume spike occurred ahead of any significant change in the underlying stock price. Moreover, unanticipated negative news in the financial sector caused market volatility to surge near the close. These dynamics underscore the value of tracking a variety of related factors, including the underlying stock, at-the-money options, and performance of the broad market.

Other position structures were also possible. Ratios have been mentioned throughout the previous chapters because they are hedged against large price swings in both directions and often completely immune to any size move in the direction of the long strike. Any of the trades in Table 3.2 could have been replaced with a ratio composed of long in-the-money calls and a larger number of short calls with the stock trading at or below the short strike price. Following this theme, we could have successfully replaced the November 2007 trade with a ratio consisting of long $160 calls and a larger number of short $170 calls. Many investors would consider this solution preferable to stopping out because it requires less attention and frees up time to monitor additional positions on other stocks. Generally speaking, strategies that require fewer adjustments and are more stable tend to deliver larger profits than high-risk positions that must be closely watched. In both scenarios, the goal is to realize profits that accrue from intraday price erosion. However, ratio trades have an additional advantage because they sometimes profit from the movement of the stock. In situations where the trade is initiated with the short side slightly out-of-the-money, a modest move of the underlying stock toward the short strike will increase the value of the long option while generating profit from the decay of the short option. As we will see, these dynamics are exaggerated as implied volatility collapse accelerates during the final few hours of expiration Friday.

Figure 3.4 outlines the performance of a replacement trade for the short straddle of Table 3.2. The new position is a 1:3 ratio consisting of long $160 calls and short $170 calls. Initial pricing was $7.15 for the long $160 call and $1.46 for the short $170 call yielding a starting price of $2.77 for the overall position. At the closing bell, the position traded for $3.93, yielding a 42% profit. The increase was driven both by a decline in the stock price and a slightly larger drop in implied volatility of the short $170 call.

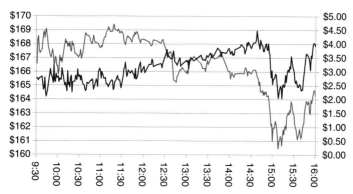

FIGURE 3.4   *Minute-by-minute value of a 1:3 ratio trade consisting of long $160 calls and short $170 calls for Apple Computer on November 15, 2007. Trading price of the ratio is displayed on the right y-axis, stock price on the left y-axis, and time on the x-axis. The dark line traces the price of the option position; the light gray line traces the stock price.*

Selecting the best combination of ratio and strike price can be complex because several different pricing dynamics come into play. These complexities, enhanced by the erratic behavior of the stock, made the November 2007 example a stringent test of any trading strategy. It was selected for this discussion specifically to highlight these issues. Overall, the trade was an excellent compromise between risk and return. It was well hedged against the large price decline that occurred in the final hour of trading, but would also have delivered a profit had the stock risen from its opening price of $166.39 to close at $170. Implied volatility was 51%–52% for both sides at the open and declined to 40% for the short $170 call and 46% for the long $160 call. Enhanced by the 1:3 ratio, the 6% difference has the same effect as an 18% difference would for a simple vertical spread that is long and short the same number of contracts at the two strike prices. In addition, falling volatility disproportionately affects the far strike of a ratio even when the decline is equal on both sides.

We can further demonstrate that the trade would have continued to generate profit even if the stock had rallied to close at $170 by plugging the actual closing volatilities into a Black-Scholes calculator and resetting the final stock price to $170. With risk-free interest set at 1.5%, the calculation yields option prices of $10.14 for the long $160 call and $2.18 for the short $170 call. Under these circumstances, therefore, the position would have had a net value of $3.60 at the market close (a 30% profit).

Net delta is also an important characteristic of any trade. Call ratios that have a large net positive delta are bullish because they profit from an increase in the stock price; large net negative deltas are bearish. Despite the 1:3 ratio, the initial position was not far from delta neutral. At initiation, the long side delta was 0.82, and the short side was 0.32, yielding a net negative delta of –0.14 (0.82 – 0.32 × 3). As a result, the position was somewhat bearish, which, combined with the larger implied volatility collapse of the short side, translated into an effective hedge against the steep late-day price decline. Structuring the trade as a 1:2 ratio would have diminished the downside hedge and created a slightly bullish position with a net positive delta equal to 0.18.

We also could have created a significantly short (bearish) trade by moving to $165 for the long strike. Initial deltas for this position would have been 0.32 for the $170 short call and 0.59 for the long $165 call, yielding a net delta of –0.37 (0.59 – 0.32 × 3). Such a position would have been very well hedged against the late-day downward spike but dangerously short during the early-morning $2 price increase. This effect is apparent in Figure 3.5, which traces minute-by-minute position value using these parameters.

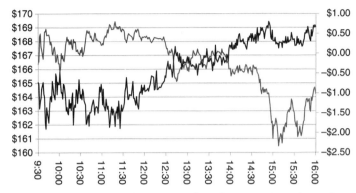

FIGURE 3.5   *Minute-by-minute value of a 1:3 ratio trade consisting of long $165 calls and short $170 calls for Apple Computer on November 15, 2007. Trading price of the ratio is displayed on the right y-axis, stock price on the left y-axis, and time on the x-axis. The dark line traces the price of the option position; the light gray line traces the stock price.*

The time frame between 9:30 and 12:00 is marked by destructive large swings in the overall position value. At initiation the trade was slightly short –$0.73. The value fell quickly to –$1.90 at 9:41 and rallied back to –$0.80 at 12:00. These large price swings resulted from a substantially negative delta layered upon an initial position value of only –$0.73. Theoretical price calculations yield position values of –$1.15 for a $1 underlying price increase, and –$1.68 for a $2 increase. (Constant implied volatility and no additional time decay are assumed.) Not surprisingly, these dynamics buffered the trade against the large downward spike of the final hour. By the closing bell, the net position value rose to +$0.67 (a 192% profit). The overall price decline and implied volatility collapse combined to yield a perfectly delta neutral position (0.15 for the short $170 call, 0.45 for the long $165 call).

Practically speaking, the $165/$170 ratio was a poorly structured trade because a bearish investor could have accomplished the same goal by simply purchasing puts with a delta of –0.37 or shorting similarly priced calls. Most conservative investors would have been forced to close the trade during one of the early large price swings. That said, the position would have generated a steady rising profit if it were initiated after the stock peaked at 11:30. Unlike a simple short position, it was immune to the $3 spike that occurred during the final 30 minutes of trading.

Simultaneously Profiting from Stock Movement and Volatility Decay

Accelerating option price decay combined with favorable underlying stock movements often generates very large returns for well-structured positions. As we have seen, call ratios are excellent examples because they are composed of a long side that can benefit from upward price movement of the stock and a short side that provides a hedge against an underlying price decline. If the stock rises, the long side gains faster than the short side, which is further out-of-the-money and suffers disproportionate value decay when implied volatility shrinks.

These dynamics allow an investor to capture most, if not all, of the impending overnight time decay without the risk of an overnight position.

One of the best trade structures involves long and short options that are both out-of-the-money with the long strike just above the stock price. Figure 3.6 depicts a trade that was constructed along these guidelines using Google call options on expiration Thursday 2008/08/14. With the stock trading at $497.70 the initial position was long $500 calls and short three times as many $510 calls. As the stock price climbed, implied volatility collapse disproportionately impacted the value of the short $510 calls. At the closing bell, with the stock at $505.17, the long $500 calls traded for nearly twice their opening price, whereas the short side gained just 14%. These changes yielded a profit of 226% as the trade value climbed from $1.20 to $3.91.

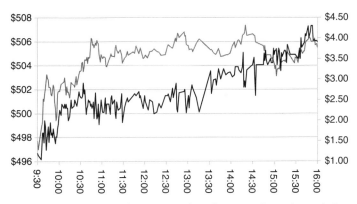

FIGURE 3.6 *Minute-by-minute value of a 1:3 ratio trade consisting of long $500 calls and short $510 calls for Google on August 14, 2008. Trading price of the ratio is displayed on the right y-axis, stock price on the left y-axis, and time on the x-axis. The dark line traces the price of the option position; the light gray line traces the price of the stock price.*

With regard to resistance against a price decline, the trade had a maximum downside risk of $1.20—the initial position cost. However, that risk would never have been realized as a loss because, had the stock fallen, the long side could have been closed, reduced in size, or replaced with stock to be held against additional short call sales. Other responses to a sharp price decline might have included purchasing longer-term put options or shorting stock. In this regard, it is important to note that the short side of the trade consisted of calls that were more than $12 out-of-the-money and losing value quickly. These dynamics allowed the creation of a trade that, despite its bullish nature, was nearly delta neutral at initiation. Table 3.4 summarizes various parameters that describe the initial and final positions.

The impact of expiration week pricing dynamics becomes apparent when implied volatilities at the close are replaced with those of the opening position initiated at 9:30. Table 3.5 extends the data of Table 3.4 with these additional values.

Had this trade been placed earlier in the expiration cycle, it would have generated the 25% loss depicted in the Net Value column. The culprit would have been stable implied volatility superimposed on a 1:3 ratio and a $7.79 stock price increase. Although the actual example involved a net delta increase from +0.03 to +0.11, the adjusted position suffered a large net delta loss from +0.03 to −0.28. In summary, the collapsing volatility trade of expiration week continued gaining value as the price of the stock climbed above the long strike, whereas the constant volatility trade lost value.

TABLE 3.4 Opening and Closing Pricing Parameters Including Implied Volatility and Delta for the Google 2008/08/14 Trade Outlined in Figure 3.4 (Volatility and delta calculations are based on a risk-free interest rate of 1.5%.)

Time	Stock ($)	Option	Option Price ($)	Implied Volat.	Delta	Net Value ($)
9:30	497.70	$500 Call	3.30	0.26	0.42	
9:30	497.70	$510 Call	0.70	0.25	0.13	1.20
16:00	505.49	$500 Call	6.32	0.17	0.80	
16:00	505.49	$510 Call	0.87	0.15	0.24	3.71

TABLE 3.5 Extensions to Table 3.4, Including Opening and Closing Pricing Parameters, with Closing Implied Volatilities Restored to Their Original 9:30 Values (The first two pairs of entries are unchanged from Table 3.4; the third pair [boldface type] contains the adjusted values. As before, volatility and delta calculations are based on a risk-free interest rate of 1.5%.)

Time	Stock ($)	Option	Option Price ($)	Implied Volat.	Delta	Net Value ($)
9:30	497.70	$500 Call	3.30	0.26	0.42	
9:30	497.70	$510 Call	0.70	0.25	0.13	1.20
16:00	505.49	$500 Call	6.32	0.17	0.80	
16:00	505.49	$510 Call	0.87	0.15	0.24	3.71
16:00	**505.49**	**$500 Call**	**7.50**	**0.26**	**0.71**	
16:00	**505.49**	**$510 Call**	**2.20**	**0.25**	**0.33**	**0.90**

Finally, it is often helpful to visualize minute-by-minute data using a sliding window that averages a small number of minutes. This simple technique erases inconsistencies that arise from momentary misalignments between highly liquid stocks and less-liquid options. Figure 3.7 displays the same data as Figure 3.6 using 3-minute moving averages for both stock and option prices.

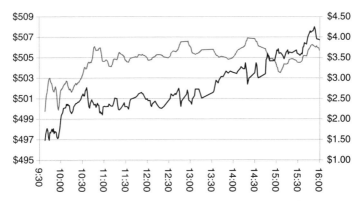

FIGURE 3.7   *Minute-by-minute value of a 1:3 ratio trade consisting of long $500 calls and short $510 calls for Google on August 14, 2008. Trading price of the ratio is displayed on the right y-axis, stock price on the left y-axis, and time on the x-axis. The dark line traces the price of the option position; the light gray line traces the stock price. Both lines are smoothed using a 3-minute moving average.*

The trend is easier to spot in the smoothed version because much noise has been removed. We can further simplify this view by creating a trendline that describes the position's behavior with a line defined by a complex polynomial. This trendline has a general form that mirrors the implied volatility collapse curve of expiration

Friday described in Chapter 1. Figure 3.8 displays the same image as Figure 3.7 superimposed on a trendline generated by Excel's charting software using a 6-degree polynomial.

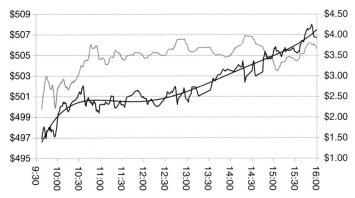

FIGURE 3.8 *Data of Figure 3.7 extended with a trendline. The form of the trendline mirrors the implied volatility collapse curves described in Chapter 1, including a midday region where volatility is relatively stable.*

The flat region of the curve that appears between 10:30 and 13:00 is related to stabilization of both the stock price and implied volatility. After 13:00, however, profit accrues more quickly, and the curve rises steadily despite a falling stock price. This dynamic strongly supports the view that collapsing implied volatility drives pricing because the position, which was net long, continued gaining value toward the close even when the underlying stock price declined. As we will see, these dynamics are dramatically exaggerated on expiration day.

Overnight Trading: Thursday–Friday

As we have seen, implied volatility tends to collapse near the close on Thursday as the market anticipates and compensates for impending overnight time decay. Sometimes the market is very efficient and Thursday's closing prices exactly equal those that would occur the next morning, with the stock trading at the same price and implied volatility restored to previous levels. In many instances, however, volatility collapse occurs on Thursday, but prices do not rebound on Friday. This exact scenario played out for the Google trade described in the previous section. Kept open until the next morning, the trade generated even more profit because implied volatility remained at depressed levels. Table 3.6 continues the analysis of this position by extending Table 3.4 with Friday morning prices.

As revealed in Table 3.6, the stock opened Friday morning $1.50 higher than Thursday's close, with call options continuing to trade at depressed implied volatilities. Overnight time decay, therefore, had a significant effect on the new $510 call price, which would have otherwise risen more than $0.35 based on the previous closing delta of 0.24. Had volatility returned to levels seen at the preceding day's open, prices would have changed dramatically. Table 3.7 continues the analysis by inserting these theoretical prices.

TABLE 3.6 Extensions to Table 3.4, Including Pricing Parameters for the Open on Expiration Friday (The first two pairs of entries are unchanged from Table 3.4; the third pair contains values for the position on Friday 2008/08/15 at 9:30. As before, volatility and delta calculations are based on a risk-free interest rate of 1.5%.)

Date	Time	Stock ($)	Option	Option Price ($)	Implied Volat.	Delta	Net Value ($)
2008/08/14	9:30	497.70	$500 Call	3.30	0.26	0.42	
2008/08/14	9:30	497.70	$510 Call	0.70	0.25	0.13	1.20
2008/08/14	16:00	505.49	$500 Call	6.32	0.17	0.80	
2008/08/14	16:00	505.49	$510 Call	0.87	0.15	0.24	3.71
2008/08/15	9:30	506.99	$500 Call	7.02	0.00	1.00	
2008/08/15	9:30	506.99	$510 Call	0.90	0.15	0.28	4.32

TABLE 3.7 Extensions to Table 3.6, Including Pricing New Parameters for the Open on Expiration Friday Calculated with Implied Volatility Restored to Previous Levels (The first three pairs of entries are unchanged from Table 3.6; the fourth pair [boldface type] contains the adjusted values. As before, volatility and delta calculations are based on a risk-free interest rate of 1.5%.)

Date	Time	Stock ($)	Option	Option Price ($)	Implied Volat.	Delta	Net Value ($)
2008/08/14	9:30	497.70	$500 Call	3.30	0.26	0.42	
2008/08/14	9:30	497.70	$510 Call	0.70	0.25	0.13	1.20
2008/08/14	16:00	505.49	$500 Call	6.32	0.17	0.80	
2008/08/14	16:00	505.49	$510 Call	0.87	0.15	0.24	3.71
2008/08/15	9:30	506.99	$500 Call	7.02	0.00	1.00	
2008/08/15	9:30	506.99	$510 Call	0.90	0.15	0.28	4.32
2008/08/15	**9:30**	**506.99**	**$500 Call**	**8.03**	**0.26**	**0.80**	
2008/08/15	**9:30**	**506.99**	**$510 Call**	**2.14**	**0.25**	**0.37**	**1.61**

Net position values displayed in the rightmost column reveal the potential impact of holding a position containing a large short component overnight. Restored implied volatility coupled with a 1:3 ratio and a modest increase in the stock price eliminated nearly all the profit generated on Thursday. Furthermore, it would have been difficult to structure a different trade at the close on Thursday because the stock traded between two strike prices.

It might seem reasonable to place trades near the close that are fully hedged against moves in the wrong direction and designed to generate profit from modest price increases. Unfortunately, if a trade is fully hedged with a substantial short component, it will tend to lose money in a rising volatility environment. Such a trade would exaggerate the dynamics observed in Table 3.7. Alternatively, reducing the size of the short component in anticipation of an opening volatility spike eliminates the hedge leaving the trade unprotected against a move in the wrong direction. Moreover, selling naked straddles or strangles in an attempt to capitalize on overnight time decay is very dangerous, and purchasing straddles in anticipation that volatility will rise enough to offset overnight time decay is an unproven strategy at best. With regard to the latter, better opportunities almost always present themselves on expiration Friday after option prices stabilize.

The advantage of well-structured hedged positions over simple short straddles or strangles becomes apparent when the underlying stock moves up or down. Even small changes can offset the value realized from time decay or implied volatility collapse. Table 3.8 helps build this case by displaying the values for simple short positions constructed around the August 2008 Google expiration that we have been discussing. Two different trades are shown. The first is a $500 short straddle opened on Thursday morning at 9:30 and closed at 16:00. The second is an overnight trade consisting of short $510 calls and $500 puts initiated at the market close on Thursday and repurchased at the opening bell Friday morning. The two trades are separated by a gray bar in the center of the table.

Each of the trades was profitable. Thursday's intraday short $500 straddle grew by 17%, and the overnight short strangle gained 25%. Corresponding values for the 1:3 ratio were 209% (intraday) and 16% (overnight). In summary, the profit potential of a simple short straddle or strangle is capped by the magnitude of the implied volatility collapse whereas trades consisting of short and long components have a directional component that can generate significant profit—in this case more than 200%. Furthermore, the $500 short straddle which was somewhat asymmetric at initiation (deltas were 0.42 and -0.58) benefited from movement in the direction of the smaller delta—that is, the put side lost value faster than the call side gained. Had the stock fallen, this asymmetry would have generated a significant loss. Ratios rarely suffer from symmetry problems because the number of contracts on each side can be fine-tuned. In this case a 1:3 ratio was very close to delta neutral. However, it is always possible to alter the ratio, add additional contracts at a third strike, or buy/sell puts to adjust a call ratio or calls to adjust a put ratio.

TABLE 3.8   Two Short Positions Designed to Take Advantage of Option Price Erosion During the August 2008 Expiration (The first is a $500 short straddle opened and closed on Thursday 2008/8/14 as a day trade [above the gray bar]. The second is a $510/$500 short strangle initiated at the closing bell on Thursday and held overnight until the opening bell on Friday morning [below the gray bar]. As before, volatility and delta calculations are based on a risk-free interest rate of 1.5%.)

Date	Time	Stock($)	Option	Option Price($)	Implied Volat.	Delta	Net Value($)
2008/08/14	9:30	497.70	$500 Call	3.30	0.26	0.42	
2008/08/14	9:30	497.70	$500 Put	5.40	0.25	-0.58	-8.70
2008/08/14	16:00	505.49	$500 Call	6.32	0.17	0.80	
2008/08/14	16:00	505.49	$500 Put	0.87	0.18	-0.21	-7.19
2008/08/14	16:00	505.49	$510 Call	0.87	0.15	0.24	
2008/08/14	16:00	505.49	$500 Put	0.87	0.18	-0.21	-1.74
2008/08/15	9:30	506.99	$510 Call	0.90	0.15	0.28	
2008/08/15	9:30	506.99	$500 Put	0.40	0.19	-0.13	-1.30

Finally, the more profitable overnight trade was nearly symmetrical at initiation with deltas of 0.24 and –0.21; both contracts traded for $0.87. The position gained 25% because implied volatility remained depressed, time decay eroded the value of the $510 calls, and the upward stock movement left the puts nearly $8 out-of-the-money with only a few hours remaining before expiration. Using the same volatilities, we can calculate an upper break-even point of $508.75—just $1.76 higher than the actual Friday opening price. The lower break-even point would have been $501.90. In summary, if the stock climbed more than $3.26 or fell more than $3.59 between Thursday's close and Friday's open, the short $510/$500 strangle would have lost money. More significantly, had implied volatility returned to Thursday morning levels (26% call/25% put), the trade would have lost 71% even if the stock remained at Thursday's closing price of $505.49. Although it might seem counterintuitive, overnight naked short straddles and strangles are risky on expiration eve.

Expiration Friday

In the first chapter, we discussed three major forces: implied volatility collapse, strike price effects, and rapidly accelerating time decay. Any option that remains out-of-the-money on expiration Friday must necessarily lose all its value by the closing bell. Conversely, very inexpensive out-of-the-money options that have just a few hours left before expiration can triple in value within a few moments if they cross a strike price. These two generalizations sum up the opportunities on expiration Friday.

One significant difference between expiration Friday and Thursday is the opportunity to profit from briefly held long straddles. The reasons are straightforward: Strike price effects often cause large discreet moves as institutional traders unwind and create new positions at different strikes, and option prices are low but stable during the midday implied volatility stabilization described in Chapter 1. Timing in this regard is important because initiating a long trade at the open or very late in the day can be dangerous because both are commonly characterized by rapidly falling implied volatility. In addition, when a stock trades near a strike price, the closing hour is often distorted by unusually small price changes.

Long straddles present many advantages: They require no excess collateral, decay at a steady and predictable rate, have limited loss potential, and, most important of all, they profit from large unanticipated price changes. Figure 3.9 illustrates these concepts with an expiration day example that was strongly driven by strike price effects. On this particular day, Research in Motion opened at $101.48 and immediately fell to $99.70 before climbing sharply to a high above $105. At the market close, the stock was pinned to the $105 strike price.

Rapidly falling implied volatility near the open stabilized the straddle price while the stock climbed from $100 to $102. The end of this time frame is marked by an arrow in the figure. At this point, implied volatility stabilized, and the rising stock price became the dominant force generating very large profits for the straddle.

Once the stock crossed the $105 strike, pinning became
the dominant force, and short straddles, covered calls or
puts, calendar spreads, ratios, or any other trade
designed to profit from a decay of a short component
would have been the best choice. Waiting for volatility
to stabilize before buying the straddle and closing the
trade at 16:00 with the stock pinned to the strike price
yielded approximately 67%. (The straddle would have
cost approximately $3.00 and sold for $5.00 at the closing bell.) This estimate is conservative because the trade
could have been purchased for less than $2.50 just a few
minutes before the arrow, and closed for more than
$5.50 at the high. Both prices persisted for some time.

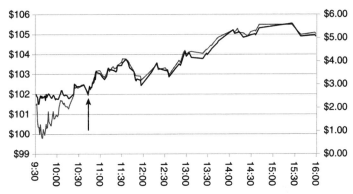

FIGURE 3.9 *Expiration day long $100 straddle for Research in
Motion (2008/03/20). Trading price of the straddle is displayed on
the right y-axis, stock price on the left y-axis, and time on the x-axis.
The dark line traces the price of the option position; the light gray
line traces the stock price. The arrow marks a point where the straddle price began rising sharply after implied volatility stabilized.*

Long straddles can also be successfully traded on stocks that display high levels of activity after a long calm period—even when this activity occurs late in the day in the window of rapidly collapsing implied volatility. Figure 3.10 displays an example using the same stock (RIMM) on a day when the price initially stabilized at one strike price ($110) and then decoupled from the strike and climbed sharply to the next higher level ($115). As previously mentioned, discreet jumps from one strike to another are common occurrences on expiration day. For an investor trading long straddles, these changes can become true sources of value creation.

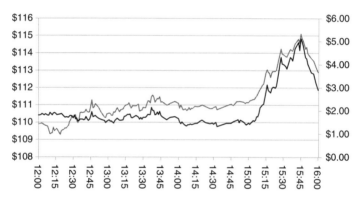

FIGURE 3.10   *Expiration day long $110 straddle for Research in Motion (2008/07/18). Trading price of the straddle is displayed on the right y-axis, stock price on the left y-axis, and time on the x-axis. The dark line traces the price of the option position; the light gray line traces the stock price. The stock decoupled from the $110 strike late in the day and rapidly jumped $5.00 to cross the $115 strike. The straddle generated more than 230% of profit.*

A second decoupling occurred at 15:45, when the stock fell away from the $115 strike to close at $112.85. No pinning behavior was apparent as the price briefly touched $115 and immediately fell away. A simple strategy for trading this scenario is to enter an order to purchase the $115 straddle for a predetermined aggressively low price. If the trade executes and the stock remains at the strike price for more than a couple of minutes, the position can be closed for a very small loss. However, if the stock crosses the strike and continues climbing or falls sharply away, the trade will generate a very large profit. In this instance, an order to purchase the $115 straddle for $0.50 would have executed at 15:45 and generated a 400% profit just a few minutes later. The full profit would have been realized because the stock never reversed direction and there was no reason to stop out before the very end of the session.

Straddles are most profitable when a stock appears to be in constant motion. We can use the same trading strategy as we did for the final decoupling of RIMM in the previous example—that is, enter an order to purchase both sides of a long straddle when the stock crosses a strike and pricing of the two sides is symmetrical. Figure 3.11 outlines the behavior of a representative trade that was executed using this strategy for MasterCard on a day when the stock's behavior was noticeably unstable throughout most of the day (2008/03/20).

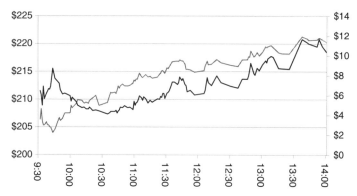

FIGURE 3.11   *Expiration day long $210 straddle for MasterCard (2008/03/20). Trading price of the straddle is displayed on the right y-axis, stock price on the left y-axis, and time on the x-axis. The dark line traces the price of the option position; the light gray line traces the stock price.*

MasterCard crossed the symmetrical entry point for a $210 straddle during the early part of the midday stable volatility window at 10:21. At a point of symmetry, the $210 straddle traded for $4.45. The stock then climbed sharply, and at 13:54 the position was closed for $11.65 with the stock trading at $221.06. Once again, strike price effects dominated, and the stock traded near the $220 strike until the close. Overall profit was 162%.

Surprisingly, on expiration Friday it is often possible to close a profitable trade, reverse strategies, and generate a second large profit using the same stock. The March 2008 MasterCard expiration serves as a perfect example because after the long straddle was closed at

13:54, the stock fell back to the $220 strike, creating a new opportunity for a short $220 straddle. A short position is an excellent choice whenever a stock climbs from one strike to another late on expiration Friday, crosses the new strike, then falls back and stabilizes. At 14:16, another point of symmetry, the $220 straddle traded for $2.70. With the stock hovering near the strike price for the remainder of the day, the straddle price decayed to $0.45. An investor who traded a long $210 straddle early in the day and a short $220 straddle late in the day would have generated two profits equal to 162% and 83% respectively. These dynamics fit well with the implied volatility profile and late day strike price effects described in Chapter 1. More specifically, the long straddle was purchased during the midday stability window when implied volatility was relatively steady and the stock was active. The short straddle was sold late in the day after the stock had gravitated to a strike price and implied volatility was collapsing. The trades were related because strike price effects drove the discreet jump from $210 to $220 that ultimately generated both profits.

Although the profit potential of long straddles on expiration day is enormous, implied volatility collapse and strike price effects are still dominant forces that can be used to generate profit from the same trade structures used on expiration Thursday. Building on our previous discussion, we can continue the Google trade described in Tables 3.4 through 3.7 to the market close on Friday. Details are displayed in Table 3.9, which extends Table 3.7 with final values for the position.

TABLE 3.9   Extensions to Table 3.7 That Complete the 1:3 Ratio Trade (The first three pairs of entries are unchanged from Table 3.7; the fourth pair contains final values at the close on expiration Friday. As before, volatility and delta calculations are based on a risk-free interest rate of 1.5%.)

Date	Time	Stock ($)	Option	Option Price ($)	Implied Volat.	Delta	Net Value ($)
2008/08/14	9:30	497.70	$500 Call	3.30	0.26	0.42	
2008/08/14	9:30	497.70	$510 Call	0.70	0.25	0.13	1.20
2008/08/14	16:00	505.49	$500 Call	6.32	0.17	0.80	
2008/08/14	16:00	505.49	$510 Call	0.87	0.15	0.24	3.71
2008/08/15	9:30	506.99	$500 Call	7.02	0.00	1.00	
2008/08/15	9:30	506.99	$510 Call	0.90	0.15	0.28	4.32
2008/08/15	16:00	510.15	$500 Call	10.22	0.00	1.00	
2008/08/15	16:00	510.15	$510 Call	0.18	0.01	0.74	9.68

Once again, a discreet price change rapidly moved the stock from one strike to the next, where strike price effects became dominant, locking in a large profit. In addition, implied volatility collapse was responsible for smoothing out the return as the value of the short $510 calls decayed rapidly enough to more than offset the effect of the rising stock price. Figure 3.12 displays the behavior of the trade on expiration Friday.

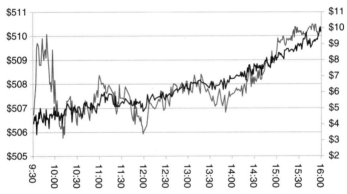

FIGURE 3.12   *Minute-by-minute value of a 1:3 ratio trade consisting of long $500 calls and short $510 calls for Google on expiration Friday 2008/08/15. This chart extends Figure 3.6, which depicts the same trade on expiration Thursday. Trading price of the ratio is displayed on the right y-axis, stock price on the left y-axis, and time on the x-axis. The dark line traces the price of the option position; the light gray line traces the stock price.*

The profile displayed in Figure 3.12 is somewhat different from that of the same trade on the preceding day (Figure 3.6). Price decay was initially rapid, causing the ratio value to rise from $4 to $6 during the first 1.5 hours. Between 11:00 and 13:00, the trade price changed only a small amount, oscillating within a range between $5 and $6. Toward the end of the day, beginning at 13:30, the price climbed steeply from just over $6 to $10. More precisely, the trade could have been initiated at 13:33 for $6.15 and unwound at 15:59, 1 minute before the closing bell, for $10.05. The time frame, therefore, generated $3.90 in 2 hours 26 minutes (a profit of 63%).

It is also noteworthy that the underlying stock price oscillations visible near the left side of the chart had little effect on the value of the ratio. In this regard, hedged trades tend to perform better than purely short positions that are sometimes closed on a transient spike to guard against a loss. In addition, because both sides of the ratio generated significant profit, it may not be meaningful to think of the trade as either a long position hedged against downward spikes or a short position hedged with long options. In actuality, both views are correct.

Finally, the ratio trade was used as an example because it contains both long and short components that each respond to implied volatility changes and time decay. Many other trade structures are possible, including covered calls, calendar spreads, and more complex multipart trades. Had we structured a covered call position, profit would have been generated both from the rising stock and collapsing value of the short $510 calls. Structuring the trade with additional short options would have generated more profit in this particular example because the $510 calls expired at the strike price. However, stock and option trades generally underperform their pure option counterparts when used in this context. Long options are superior to stock because their cost can be nearly or completely covered by the short option sale. Such positions are protected against any size move in the out-of-the-money direction. Pure option positions are also superior to stock and option positions because the delta of the long side can rise to accommodate a large spike in the direction of the strike price. Conversely, stock is equivalent to an option with a delta of 1.0—that is, a deep in-the-money option. Positions structured with stock must therefore be adjusted more often if the goal is to stay within a particular net delta range. Complex multipart trades and trades that span different time frames tend to add unnecessary complexity in the context of a day trading strategy. However, investors have different goals that may be accommodated by more complex structures. For example, it is completely reasonable to purchase options with distant expirations and to offset the time decay of these contracts by selling at-the-money options each month during expiration. Similar strategies have traditionally involved a series of short positions that decay across the time frame of an entire month. However, replacing monthly short positions with expiration day trades will usually generate more profit in a shorter time with limited market exposure.

Appendix 1

Excel VBA Program for Counting Strike Price Crosses

Following is an Excel VBA program that tabulates strike price crosses for a single stock. Individual records can span any timeframe—minute, hour, day, and so on. Each row is assumed to contain a new record with columns A-G organized as follows: A=Symbol, B=Date/Time, C=Open, D=High, E=Low, F=Close, and G=Volume. Only columns D (High) and E (Low) are critical to the operation of the program. Three additional columns are automatically created: H=Crosses, I=Total, and J=Average.

The program also refers to a second worksheet containing a single column of strike prices (column A). A working copy of this data is created in the worksheet being tabulated. The working copy is automatically deleted when the program exits.

All strikes touched by the stock are counted, including those that exactly equal the low or high of each record. Results are stored in column H (Crosses) and tabulated in column I (Total) and column J (Average).

A sample output is included following the program listing for reference. Although the sample contains just 10 records, the program can process listings as long as 100,000 records in just a few seconds.

```
Sub Strike_Crosses_1stock()

Dim Sheet_1 As String
Dim Row As Long

Dim CurrentHigh As Double
Dim CurrentLow As Double
Dim HighStrike As Double
Dim LowStrike As Double
Dim HighStrikeRow As Integer
Dim LowStrikeRow As Integer
Dim Sum As Double
Dim Divisor As Double

On Error GoTo ProgramExit

'store coordinates for current worksheet
Sheet_1 = ActiveCell.Worksheet.name
Row = ActiveCell.Row
Column = ActiveCell.Column

'retrieve strike prices
Sheets("strikes").Select
Columns("A:A").Select
Selection.Copy
Sheets(Sheet_1).Select
Range("K1").Select
ActiveSheet.Paste
```

```
'new column headings
Cells(1, "H") = "Crosses"
Cells(1, "I") = "Total"
Cells(1, "J") = "Average"

'initialize variables
Sum = 0
Divisor = 0
Row = 2

'Main program logic
While Cells(Row, "A") <> ""

'capture high, low
CurrentHigh = Cells(Row, "D")
CurrentLow = Cells(Row, "E")

'Row 2 is a starting point with
'the highest possible strike price
HighStrikeRow = 2

'locate high strike price
While Cells(HighStrikeRow, "K") > CurrentHigh
HighStrikeRow = HighStrikeRow + 1
Wend
HighStrike = Cells(HighStrikeRow, "K")

'locate low strike price
LowStrikeRow = HighStrikeRow
While Cells(LowStrikeRow, "K") >= CurrentLow
LowStrikeRow = LowStrikeRow + 1
Wend
LowStrikeRow = LowStrikeRow - 1
LowStrike = Cells(LowStrikeRow, "K")

'store result for record  in column H
'store blank if no strikes are crossed
Cells(Row, "H") = LowStrikeRow - HighStrikeRow + 1
If Cells(Row, "H") < 1 Then
Cells(Row, "H") = ""
End If
```

```
'increment sum and row count
Sum = Sum + Cells(Row, "H")
Divisor = Divisor + 1

'move to next record
Row = Row + 1
Wend

'store total strike crosses in column I
'store average in column J
Cells(2, "I") = Sum
Cells(2, "J") = Sum / Divisor

ProgramExit:

'Delete Strike Column
Columns("K:K").Select
Selection.Delete Shift:=xlToLeft

'return to upper left cell
Range("A1").Select

End Sub
```

Sample program output for 10 daily records:

Symbol	Day	O	H	L	C	Volume	Crosses	Total	Average
XXX	20081215	122.01	123.50	119.82	122.06	426705	1	18	1.80
XXX	20081216	123.45	125.03	119.11	123.00	406622	2		
XXX	20081217	123.45	128.45	120.01	126.34	461139	1		
XXX	20081218	127.00	132.56	126.00	131.56	494027	1		
XXX	20081219	131.67	133.34	122.65	124.12	355183	2		
XXX	20081222	125.23	126.78	115.00	118.12	615748	3		
XXX	20081223	117.67	117.89	108.98	109.23	321841	2		
XXX	20081224	108.34	108.34	97.98	98.50	324370	2		
XXX	20081225	99.45	101.45	99.00	100.01	366578	1		
XXX	20081226	102.12	105.23	94.21	94.67	273438	3		

INDEX

FINANCIAL TIMES

In an increasingly competitive world, it is quality of thinking that gives an edge—an idea that opens new doors, a technique that solves a problem, or an insight that simply helps make sense of it all.

We work with leading authors in the various arenas of business and finance to bring cutting-edge thinking and best-learning practices to a global market.

It is our goal to create world-class print publications and electronic products that give readers knowledge and understanding that can then be applied, whether studying or at work.

To find out more about our business products, you can visit us at www.ftpress.com.